THE Spurgeon

BIRTHDAY BOOK

RARE QUOTES & METAPHORS
FOR EVERY DAY OF THE YEAR

Charles Spurgeon

The Spurgeon Birthday Book
Rare Quotes & Metaphors for
Every Day of the Year
© 2020 by Charles Spurgeon
Gideon House Books

ISBN: 978-1-943133-81-9

All Scripture quotations, unless indicated, are
taken from the *Holy Bible: American Standard
Version*. Public Domain

Cover design and interior layout by
Josh Pritchard

GIDEON HOUSE BOOKS
www.gideonhousebooks.com

METAPHORS OFTEN CONVEY to the mind truth which otherwise would not have reached the understanding; for men frequently see under the guise and form of an illustration a doctrine which, if it had been nakedly stated, they could not have comprehended. Illustrations, like windows, let light into the chambers of the mind. There is this use also in a metaphor, that, even if it be not understood at first, it excites thought, and men exercise their minds upon it as children upon an enigma; and so they learn, perhaps, more through a dark saying than through a sentence transparent at first sight. Yet further: metaphorical speech is apt to abide upon the memory, it retains its hold even upon the unwilling mind, like a lion which has leaped upon a giraffe in the desert. Mere bald statement is soon forgotten, but illustrations stick in the soul like hooks in a fish's mouth.

C. H. Spurgeon

"Thoughts that breathe
and words that burn."

January 1

Another chapter in the book of love is about to open before us, and its initial letter is illuminated with hope. Hosts of angels are coming to meet us, and each one bears a blessing. We shall need new praises as we advance into the wonderland of future mercy, for every day will unfold fresh marvels of faithfulness and grace. Come then, brethren, let us sing unto the Lord a new song. Let us deck the new year's brow with a crown of grateful hope. While the bells ring forth from the church steeples, let them ring in our hearts too.

January 2

The first coating of ice is scarcely perceptible. Keep the water stirring, and you will prevent the frost from hardening it; but once you let it film over and remain quiet, the glaze thickens upon the surface, and at last it is so firm that a wagon might be drawn across the solid ice. So it is with the conscience; it films over gradually, until at last it becomes hard and unfeeling, and is not crushed even with ponderous loads of iniquity.

January 3

Beware of a growing greediness, for covetousness is one of the most insidious of sins. It is like the silting up of a river. As the stream comes down from the mountains it brings with it sand and earth and stones, and it deposits these at its mouth, until by degrees, unless the conservators watch it carefully, it will block itself up, and it will be difficult to find a channel for ships of great burden. So too are souls silted up by that which they themselves accumulate.

January 4

Communion is strength, isolation is weakness. Alone, the fine old beech yields to the blast and lies prone upon the grass: in the forest, supporting each other, the trees laugh at the hurricane. The sheep of Jesus flock together; the social element is the genius of Christianity. To find a brother is to win a pearl of great price; to retain a friend is to treasure up the gold of Ophir.

January 5

How often would deep despondencies and heavy glooms be chased away if an all absorbing love to Jesus and a fiery zeal for his honor burned within our hearts. One fire puts out another, and a grander agony of soul quenches all other griefs. The hands of holy industry pluck the canker of care from the heart, while o'er the diligent soul the Lord sheds a heavenly dew, which makes the desert of his sorrow to blossom as the rose.

January 6

Time flies with such impetuous wing that no express train can overtake it, and even the lightning flash lags behind it. A lifetime is gone or ever we are aware. We shall soon see the great white throne! We shall soon stand at the judgment seat of God! Let us be making ready for the day of days, when the Ancient of Days shall sit. Let us not live so much in the dreams of the fleeting present but let us project our lives into the realities of the eternal future.

January 7

Souls are not saved by systems, but by the Spirit. Organizations without the Holy Ghost are mills without wind, or water, or steam power. Methods and arrangements without grace are pipes from a dry conduit, lamps without oil, banks without capital. Even the most scriptural forms of church government and effort are clouds without rain till the "power from on high" be given.

January 8

When Cyrus took one of his guests into his garden, the visitor admired it greatly, and said that he had much pleasure in it. "Ah!" said Cyrus, "but you take not so much delight in this garden as I do, for I planted every tree in it myself." Our Lord takes great delight in his Church because he has done so much for it; and one reason why certain saints will have a greater fullness of heaven than others will be because they helped to bring more souls to heaven than others.

January 9

Let him go at his own pace, and my horse will invariably come back in less time than he makes the journey out. He speeds the carriage on its way with a hearty good will when his face is toward home. Should I not also both suffer and labor the more joyously because my way lies towards heaven, and my face is turned towards my Father's house above, my soul's dear home and everlasting mansion?

January 10

Look at the birds among the trees, how they shame us! Sweet little creatures, if you watch them when they are singing you will wonder how so much sound can come forth from such diminutive bodies. They throw their whole frames into the music and seem to melt themselves away in song! How the wing vibrates, the throat pulsates, and every part of the body is thrilled by the joyful strain! This is the way in which we ought to praise God.

January 11

The heart is naturally so corrupt, that love to God was never found within it until the Lord himself placed it there. Should I see a rare exotic flower smiling in a hedge-row, I should know that some garden had lent it to the rugged soil; and so is it with love to God, its seed comes from God's love to us, it springs not like a weed in the furrow, but is sown by the Lord's own hand. You may conclude, with absolute certainty, that God loves you if you love God.

January 12

Evil thoughts are the marrow of sin; the malt that sin is brewed from; the tinder which catches the sparks of the devil's temptations; the chum in which the milk of imagination is churned into purpose and plan; the nest in which all evil birds lay their eggs. Be certain, then, that as surely as fire burns brushwood as well as logs, God will punish thoughts of sin as well as deeds of sin.

January 13

Thread the jewels of Jehovah's grace upon the string of memory and hang them on the neck of praise. What a task is this for the strongest memory and the readiest reckoner! Can you count the leaves of the forest in autumn, or number the small dust of the threshing-floor? Only then can you calculate the sum of your Redeemer's loving-kindnesses. For mercies beyond measure, praise the Lord with all your effort.

January 14

Every good thing that is in a Christian, not merely begins, but progresses, and is consummated by the fostering grace of Jesus Christ. If my finger were on the golden latch of Paradise, and my foot were on its jasper threshold, I could not take the last step so as to enter its blissful abodes unless the grace which brought me so far should enable me fully and fairly to complete my pilgrimage. Jonah's sentence is full of sea-salt and of the salt of wisdom, "Salvation is of the Lord."

January 15

There is nothing little to a father in the thing that troubles his little child; and your great God, having once condescended to observe and care for you, numbering the very hairs of your head, and not suffering a sparrow to fall to the ground without his purpose and decree, will not think that you intrude upon him if you bring your daily troubles to him, even the little ones.

January 16

Oftentimes men of the world will give their money to the cause of Christ, putting down large sums for charity or for missions, but they will not weep in secret over other men's sins, or speak a word of comfort to an afflicted saint. To visit a poor sick woman, teach a little child, reclaim a homeless person, breathe a prayer for an enemy, or whisper a promise in the ear of a desponding saint, may show more of sonship than building a row of almshouses or endowing a church.

January 17

How often does my soul feel like an almost hatched chick, shut up within a narrow shell, in darkness and discomfort! The life within labors hard to chip and break the shell, to know a little more of the great universe of truth, and see in clearer light the infinite of divine love. Oh, happy day, when the shell shall be broken, and the soul, complete in the image of Christ, shall enter into the freedom for which she is preparing!

January 18

Do not imagine that you are always to be a babe in grace. You shall grow and become a man, yea, a father in Israel. Imagine not that you are always to be that slender green blade which is waving feebly out of the cold ground, you shall one day be the corn in the ear: yea, you shall one day be the golden corn which bends its head through ripeness, and the glad harvest-home shall be shouted over you.

January 19

As when the new moon first shows her slender ring of light, so the earth at this day is rimmed and edged with a divine illumination, which shall increase till the whole circle of the globe shall be irradiated, and shall in full-orbed splendor reflect the glory of God. Then, also, shall music blend with the growing brightness; light and sweetness shall be wedded again, and earth, like a lamp of God's sanctuary, and a golden bell of the high priest's garment, shall shine forth, and ring out the praises of her God.

January 20

A highlander who purchased a barometer under a mistaken idea of its purpose, complained that he could not see that it had made any improvement in the weather; and those who use signs and evidences for an intent which they will never answer, will be sure to complain that their faith is not increased, though they are always practicing self-examination. Yet a barometer has its uses, and so have evidences of grace.

January 21

Some minds are specially fertile in self-torture; they have the creative faculty for all that is melancholy, desponding, and wretched. If they were placed in the brightest isles of the blessed, beneath unclouded skies, where birds of fairest wing pour out perpetual melody, and earth is richest with color and perfume, they would not be content till they had imagined for themselves a sevenfold Styx; flowing through a valley crowded with graves and enshrouded in everlasting midnight.

January 22

There are many locks in our house and all with different keys, but we have one master key which opens all. So the Lord has many treasuries and secrets, all shut up from carnal minds with locks which they cannot open; but he who walks in fellowship with Jesus possesses the master key, which will admit him to all the blessings of the covenant.

January 23

It is well to give because you love to give; as the flower which pours forth its perfume because it never dreamed of doing otherwise; or like the bird which quivers with song because it is a bird, and finds a pleasure in its notes; or like the sun which shines, not by constraint, but because being a sun it must shine; or like the waves of the sea, which flash back the brilliance of the sun, because it is their nature to reflect and not to hoard the light.

January 24

Meditation puts the telescope to the eye, and enables us to see Jesus in a better way than we could have seen Him if we had lived in the days of His earthly sojourn; for now we see not Jesus in the flesh, but the spiritual Jesus; we see the spirit of Christ, the life and essence of Emmanuel, the very soul of the Savior. Happy is the eye which is blest with a clear spiritual sight of Jesus.

January 25

Our national music has never been so devout as it should have been, and we are poor in holy national song, as compared with the Hebrews. May the taste of coming ages improve in this respect. Let us, in the events which occur in our own time, see the hand of God, and if we cannot write psalms and hymns, yet, at any rate, let us express our glowing thanksgiving to that God who has bidden the ocean gird our native isle, and has thus protected her with a better guard than gates of brass or triple steel.

January 26

Weep not because the vessel of your present comfort has gone out to sea, and you have lost sight of its white sails; it shall come back again to you laden with nobler treasure. Weep not because the sun has gone down, for it descends so that the dews may be brought forth, that the earth may be watered and the flowers may drip with perfume. Wait a while, and the sun shall come back to you again, and the light of the morning shall be all the clearer because of the mists of the night.

January 27

King James I once said of armor, that "it was an excellent invention, for it not only saved the life of the wearer, but it hindered him from doing harm to anybody else." Equally destructive to all usefulness is that excessive prudence upon which some professors pride themselves; not only do they escape all persecution, but they are never able to strike a blow, much less to fight a battle, for the Lord Jesus.

January 28

As the hen broods her chickens under her wings, so should we cherish all holy thoughts. As the poor man's lamb ate of his own bread, and lay in his bosom, even so should godly meditation be very dear to us. Holy thoughts breed holy words and holy actions, and are hopeful evidences of a renewed heart. Will not this day afford some choice moment for contemplation? Will in not be like Peter's fish with silver in its mouth?

January 29

He who can rejoice in the promise of the resurrection, and of the life to come, dies grandly; his bed is changed into a throne; his little room, despite its poverty, becomes a palace chamber, and the child of God, who seemed so poor before, is perceived to be a peer of heaven's own blood royal, about to take possession of the heritage appointed for him from before the foundation of the world.

January 30

Give me that harp, and let my fingers never leave its strings, the harp whose chords resound the love of Christ alone. To harp upon the name of Jesus is a blessed monotony containing more variety than all other subjects combined. When Jesus is the first, the midst, the last, yea, all in all, then do we make full proof of our ministry. Lord, tune our hearts to this music!

January 31

Our heart is to be like those beacons and watchtowers which were prepared along the coast of England when the invasion of the Armada was hourly expected, not always blazing, but with the wood always dry, and the match always there, the whole pile being ready to blaze up at the appointed moment. Our souls should burst forth with prayer as naturally as our chest heaves with breath.

February 1

The man who lives by policy is like a sailor who has an unfavorable wind. He must tack about to reach first this point and then the other, and he will make but slow progress after all in the direction which he really wishes to pursue. But the man who has the life of God, and follows the way of truth, is like a gallant steam vessel which plows its way straight on, wind or tide notwithstanding, because its force is within itself.

February 2

Sometimes the heir of heaven grows impatient of his bondage, and like a captive who, looking out of the narrow window of his prison, beholds the green fields of the unfettered earth, and marks the flashing waves of the ocean, ever free, and hears the songs of the uncaged tenants of the air, weeps as he views his narrow cell, and hears the clanking of his chains. Patience, my heart, the warder comes, his key is in the door, and you shall soon be set free!

February 3

We could never have known Christ's love in all its heights and depths if he had not died; nor could we have guessed the Father's deep affection if he had not given his Son to die. The common mercies we enjoy all sing of love, just as the sea-shell, when we put it to our ear whispers of the deep from where it came; but if we desire to hear the boom of the ocean of divine love, we must not only consider everyday blessings, but the eternal blessings of Calvary.

February 4

It is said of homemade troubles that they are very like homemade clothes, they never fit well, and they generally last longer than others. Do not, therefore, create imaginary ills, for they are not easily removed. Rest content with the troubles which God sends you; they are more suitable for you than self-devised sorrows, you will be better able to carry them, and the burden will prove a blessing.

February 5

We think we ought to grow in grace through what we enjoy, but we probably make the greatest progress through what we suffer. Soft gales may be pleasant for heaven-bound vessels, but rough winds often do most to speed their voyage. The calm is our way, but God has His way in the whirlwind, and he rides on the wings of the wind. Saints often gain more by their losses than by their profits.

February 6

In nothing do men make more mistakes than concerning their own characters. I have listened to a brother confess that he was deficient in firmness, when, in my opinion, he was about as obstinate as any man I knew. Another man has said that he was always lacking in coolness, and yet I thought that if I needed to fill an ice house, I had only to put him into it. We are partial judges of ourselves. Unfeeling people say they are too sensitive, and selfish persons imagine themselves to be too generous. Weigh yourself in the balances of the sanctuary.

February 7

Defeated in one battle a commander attempts another, and hopes that he may yet win the campaign, but this, O man, you cannot do. Your life is your one battle, and if it be lost your defeat is eternal. The man who was bankrupt yesterday begins again in business with a good heart, and hopes that he may yet succeed; but in the business of this mortal life, if you are found bankrupt, you have failed forever.

February 8

The devotion of the monastery is by no means equal to that of the soldier of Christ who takes his appointed place in the battle of life. The piety of the convent and the monastery is at best the heroism of a soldier who hides behind the baggage, but the religion of the man in business life, who turns all to the glory of God, is the courage of a warrior who seeks the thickest of the fray, and there bears aloft the grand old standard of Jehovah-nissi.

February 9

On a tradesman's table I noticed a book labelled Want Book. What a practical suggestion for a man of prayer! He should write down all his needs on the tablets of his heart, and then present his want-book to God. If we knew all our need, what a large want-book we should require! How comforting to know that Jesus has a supply book which exactly meets our want book!

February 10

If soldiers can win a battle and sing sweetly at the same time, by all means let them sing, but if it so happens that while regarding the harmonies they miss a cut at their enemies, let the music come to an end at once. There, young warrior, give up the song and vault into your saddle!

February 11

The sight of weakness begets pity in a gentle mind. It is said that, when a certain town was being sacked, one of the fierce battalions spared a little child because it said, "Please, sir, don't kill me, I am so little." Did a rough warrior feel the power of this plea? Then, little one, you may yourself use this argument with God. "O God, do not destroy me! I am less than the least of all thy mercies, therefore spare thou me."

February 12

A man might stand at the stake and burn for a few minutes, but when it comes to roasting for hours before a slow fire, who can bear it? To do one brave and generous action is simple enough; but to stand on the watchtower day and night, always watching, lest the foe surprise us, or our hearts betray us; watching unto prayer, that we may keep ourselves in the love of God; this is the work, this is the labor; and only grace can help us to perform it. Aid us, O Holy Spirit!

February 13

When our glorious Lord entered into our souls, wearing his vesture dipped in blood, pardoning and blessing us in the fullness of his grace, then the bells of our heart rang merry peals; the streamers of our joy floated in the fragrant air; the streets of our soul were strewn with roses of delight; the fountains of our love ran with red wine, and our soul was as full of bliss as a heart could be this side of heaven; for salvation had come to our house, and mercy's King had deigned to visit us.

February 14

The Spaniards of Chile believed that no water was so wholesome or of so delicate a flavor as that which flowed through veins of gold: certainly no conversation is so edifying to the hearers as that which pours forth from a heart stored with sacred knowledge, sanctified experience, devout contemplation, communion with Jesus, and such like precious things. Lord, fill us with such treasure that our conversations may be heavenly.

February 15

If you would serve like an apostle, and glow like a seraph, behold the grace awaiting you in Jesus. If you would go from strength to strength, climbing the loftiest summits of holiness, behold grace upon grace prepared for you. If you are confined, it is not in Christ; if there be any bound to your holy attainments, it is set by yourself. The infinite God gives Himself to you in the person of his dear Son, and He saith to you, "All things are yours."

February 16

O the savor of the name of Jesus, when heard by the ear which has been opened by the Spirit! O the beauty of the person of Jesus, when seen with the eye of faith by the illumination of the Holy One of Israel! As the light of the morning, when the sun arises, "as a morning without clouds," is our Well-Beloved unto us. The sight of the burning bush made Moses put off his shoes, but the transporting vision of Jesus makes us put off all the world.

February 17

The songs you are yet to sing, the grapes of Eshcol you are yet to pluck, the fair days of joy you are yet to spend, should be foretasted by your hope. Snatch from the altars of the future a blazing brand with which to light up the darkness of today. Safety on earth, and after death the fullness of heaven, are our sure portion, so let us sing unto the Lord the psalm of hope.

February 18

He who, amidst a thousand troubles, keeps his heart whole and his garments white by standing firm in his integrity, may battle against all the world and all the hosts of hell, and not be afraid; but he who does ill out of policy has thrown away his shield. Innocence unarmored is yet clad in mail, while craft and fraud though sheathed in steel shall fall, fatally wounded by the arrows of eternal providence.

February 19

Heroes who have been most distinguished for fury in the fight have been tender of heart as little children; sharp were their swords to the foe, but gentle their hands towards the weak. It is the mark of a noble nature that it can be majestic as a lion in the presence of enemies, and roar like a young lion in the midst of conflict, and yet it has a dove's eye and a maiden's heart. Such is our Lord Jesus Christ; he is the conquering Captain of salvation, but he is meek and lowly of heart.

February 20

If you have wandered like Noah's dove, flying over the waste of the waters, the Lord will receive you, even as Noah received the weary bird. He put out his hand at once, and "pulled her in unto him, into the ark"; and even so does the divine Savior take us in to himself. Our wing is too weary to bear us to the ark of salvation, and we are ready to faint into the floods of despair, and then the pierced hands encompass and lift us. So is Jesus our Noah, our truest rest and rest-giver.

February 21

The bell in the steeple may be well hung, fairly fashioned, and of soundest metal, but it is silent until the ringer makes it speak; and in like manner the preacher has no voice of quickening for the dead in sin, or of comfort for living saints, until the divine Spirit gives him a gracious touch, and bids him speak with power. Lord, move each one of us to ring out thy praise.

February 22

If one little mechanical bird, with a few clockwork movements, were warbling out something like music in an exhibition, everybody would gather round it, and many would even pay to hear it sing; but though thousands of birds sing infinitely more sweetly than anything man can produce, a cruel generation is more ready to kill them than to listen to them. Men admire their own poor copies, but despise the grand originals of God.

February 23

We were awakened at six o'clock, in the Hartz mountains, by the cheerful notes of a trumpet, playing a tuneful and enlivening German air, and so proclaiming the Sabbath. It struck me that it was a fitting way to usher in the happy day of rest. I would on the Lord's day wake up with music, and conclude my sleep with a dream of angels chanting the songs of heaven, and inviting me to join their choir. Not with the dull note of the trombone, but with psaltery and harp of joyful sound, let the Sabbath dawn.

February 24

We must ourselves drink of the living water till we are full, and then out of the midst of us shall flow rivers of living water; but not till then. Out of an empty basket you cannot distribute loaves and fishes, however hungry the crowd may be. Out of an empty heart you cannot speak full things, nor from a famished soul bring forth rich things full of marrow, nor from a dead heart impart life. Be blessed that you may bless.

February 25

The old creation has its sunshine and flowers, its lowing herds and bleating flocks, its heaven-mounting larks and warbling nightingales, its rivers laughing and its floods clapping their hands; is the new creation of grace to render less happy worship to God our exceeding joy? Nay rather, let us come into his presence with thanksgiving, and show ourselves glad in him with psalms.

February 26

A man who is traveling all alone on a dark road infested by highwaymen, if he has a sword with him, will carry it drawn in his hand, to let the robbers know that he is ready for them. So must the Christian, seeing he is in an enemy's country, pray without ceasing. Carry your sword in your hand. Unsheathe the mighty weapon of all-prayer. This is the true Jerusalem blade, which will cut through coats of armor. Fear no foe if you can but pray. Satan himself trembles at the power of prayer.

February 27

The face of Jesus is more lovely to God than all the beauties of creation, his eyes are brighter than heaven, his voice is sweeter than bliss; therefore does the Father will to have his Son's beauty reflected as by ten thousand mirrors in saints made in his image, and he purposes to have his praises chanted by myriads of voices of those who love him because his blood has saved them.

February 28

Since our Lord Jesus Christ has taken away the curse of sin, a great rock has been lifted out from the river-bed of God's mercy, and the living stream comes rippling, rolling, swelling on in crystal floods, sweeping before it all human sin and sorrow, and making glad the thirsty who stoop down to drink thereat. Was it not of this river that Ezekiel prophesied, "everything that lives, which moves, wherever the rivers shall come, shall live"?

February 29

If I must choose that part of the Christian life in which there is the most joy, next to the land Beulah, which is the fairest portion of Immanuel's land by reason of its lying so near to Canaan, I would prefer that tract of godly experience which lies toward the rising of the sun, which is sown with orient pearls of love, and cheered with the delicious music of the birds of hope: it is called the land of our espousals. Here faith sits under her vine and fig-tree, and no one can make her afraid.

March 1

N old weather proverb says that if March comes in like a lion it will go out like a lamb. It is so with many other things, such as our troubles, which often threaten our unbelieving hearts, but turn to blessings in the end. Our spiritual feelings also are often at the first terrible as a lion, yet by faith in Christ Jesus the lion becomes a lamb: we begin with a sense of divine anger and end in peace with God through Jesus Christ our Lord.

March 2

Uniformity is no rule of spiritual life. Let us not censure others because their feelings have not been precisely similar to ours. The trees are not all of one form, and even in every several leaves is an original. Among the tiniest mosses no two are quite the same. God is not tied to one type or model, but his works exhibit an infinite variety.

March 3

Let no man think himself at the end of the war till he is within the pearly gate; for, if there be but another five minutes to live, Satan will, if possible, avail himself of it to do us more mischief. The enemy may come in like a flood, precisely at that flattering moment when you hoped to dwell in the land of peace, and to be lulled to rest by soft strains from the celestial choirs. "What I say unto you, I say unto all, watch."

March 4

I have never worshiped even in the presence of Mont Blanc, or amid the crash of thunder, as I have adored the Lord at the foot of the cross. A sense of goodness creates a better worshiper than a sense of the sublime. In our best seasons the grandest sublimities of nature are too small a mirror to set forth the Lord; they dwarf rather than magnify our conceptions of his glory. Jesus saith, "He that hath seen me hath seen the Father." Nowhere else is Jehovah fully revealed.

March 5

O for conquering grace to crush down self. I would be as a grain of dust blown in the summer's gale, without power to change my course, carried on by the irresistible breath of the Spirit; forever made willingly unwilling to will anything but the will of my Lord. I would be as a tiny straw carried along by the Gulf Stream, carried wherever the warm love of God shall bear me, delighting to be nothing and to see the Lord alone exalted.

March 6

What a serene and quiet life might you lead if you would leave providing to the God of providence. With a little oil in the bowl, and a handful of flour in the jar, Elijah outlived the famine, and you will do the same. If God cares for you, why need you care too? Can you trust him for your soul, and not for your body? He has never refused to bear your burdens, he has never fainted under their weight, why then stagger under them yourself?

March 7

Almost all Asian houses are very dark, and if anything be dropped as small as a piece of silver, it must be looked for with a candle even at high noon. Now, the sphere in which the church moves on earth is a dim twilight of mental ignorance and moral darkness, and in order to find a lost soul light must be brought to bear upon it. Let us never sweep the house for the Lord's lost ones without first knowing well the Gospel for ourselves. We can do nothing in the dark. Enlighten our darkness, good Lord.

March 8

The common run of human faith is fair-weather faith: a faith which loves to see its own idolized image mirrored in the glassy wave, but is far away when the storm clouds are marshaling for battle. The faith of God's elect is the faith that can see in the dark, the faith that is calm in the tumult, the nightingale faith which can sing among thorns, the faith which shines like a lone star when everything around her is black as midnight.

March 9

Only the living faith which works upon the heart, and influences the desires and the affections, can be the faith of God's elect. A moonlight faith, which has light but no warmth, is a thing of the night, and is not the faith of the children of the day. Faith which lives in the cold attic of the brain, and never descends into the parlor and banqueting room of the heart, will starve with cold; and it is not the faith which the Holy Spirit works in man.

March 10

When a traveler was asked whether he did not admire the admirable structure of some stately building, he said "No, for I have been to Rome, where better things are to be seen every day." O believer, if the world tempts you with its rare sights and curious prospects, you ought scorn them, having been, by contemplation, in heaven, and being able by faith to see infinitely better delights every hour of the day.

March 11

Many horses fall at the bottom of a hill because the driver thinks the danger past and the need to hold the reins with firm grip less pressing. So is it often with us when we are not specially tempted to overt sin, we are the more in danger through slothful ease. I think it was Ralph Erskine who said, "No temptation is so bad as not being tempted." Lord, even when we are not in temptation, we will still pray "deliver us from evil"!

March 12

Have you ever noticed how badly boys write at the bottom of the pages in their copy-books? There is the copy at the top, and in the first line they look at their teacher's writing; in the second line they copy their own imitation; in the third line they follow their copy of their imitation, and so the writing grows worse and worse as it descends the page. We shall do the same if we do not constantly keep our eye on Jesus himself, who is our sole Exemplar.

March 13

Plutarch tells us of two men at Athens who were nominated for a public office. One of them was famous for his oratory skills, and to gain the election he gave a description of what he could and would do if the citizens would choose him. He would have charmed them with his fine promises, but they knew him too well. His rival was a man of few words, and simply said, "All that this gentleman has said I mean to do." A holy life is better than pious talk.

March 14

From the deck of an Austrian gunboat we threw into the Lago Garda a succession of little pieces of bread, and presently small fishes came in shoals, till there seemed to be, as the old proverb puts it, more fish than water. They came to feed and needed no music. Flock then around the preacher who gives his people food, even if he does not possess the sounding brass of rhetoric and the tinkling cymbals of oratory.

March 15

The way to heaven is downhill as to yourself. As Christ went down to the grave that he might come up again and fulfill all things, so must you go down to his cross, and down to his grave, and self must be dead and buried with Christ. Then will you learn the meaning of your baptism, and make it true that you are buried with him to all the world, and to yourself also, for so only can you rise into fullness of life.

March 16

The church is God's shelter, where he distributes bread and wine to refresh the weary, and entertains wayfarers that else had been lost in the storm. The church is God's hospital, into which he takes the sick, and there he nourishes them till they renew their youth like the eagles. It is God's great lighthouse with its lantern flashing forth a directing ray so that wanderers far away may be directed to the haven of peace. But mind, it must be God's church, and not man's.

March 17

Temporal mercies without Christ are like numbers without a figure, but when Jesus stands in front of them, what an amount they make! Temporal mercies without Christ are unripe fruit, but when Christ shines upon them, they grow mellow and sweet. Temporal mercies without Christ are as a landscape without the sun, but when Jesus lights them up how beautiful they become as tokens of divine love. Truly "Christ is all and in all."

March 18

Sometimes the sun is up before you know whether it has risen or not, because a long morning twilight precedes its actual appearance above the horizon. So it may be that spiritual life dawns by slow degrees, before we quite perceive it in our souls; but yet there is a time when it begins. There is a point at which the unsaved become saved, and the unregenerate become regenerate; and there is a broad line between the two characters. On which side are you?

March 19

Does Jesus love me? Does he seal the fact by declaring it with his own lips? Then I will not make stipulations with him as to his dealings with me. If he loves me he must act towards me with loving-kindness; he will not strike his beloved unless love dictates the blow; he will not forsake his chosen, for he never changes. Oh, the inexpressible blessedness of the man who knows in his own soul that the heavenly Bridegroom calls him his beloved!

March 20

Bunyan tells us that Mercy laughed in her sleep; and no wonder, when she dreamed of Jesus. My joy shall not stop short of hers while my Beloved is the theme of my daily thoughts. The Lord Jesus is a great sea of delight; my soul shall dive into the depths of Christ's own joy. Sarah looked on her Isaac, and laughed with pleasure, and all her friends laughed with her; and you, my soul, look on your Lord and bid heaven and earth unite in your unspeakable joy.

March 21

No flowers wear so lovely a blue as those which grow at the foot of the frozen glacier; no stars gleam so brightly as those which glisten in the polar sky; no fountain is so sweet as that which springs amid the desert sand; and no faith is so precious as that which lives and triumphs in adversity. "Lord, I believe. Help me in my unbelief."

March 22

Kindness, benevolence, and generosity are essential to the perfect character; to be strictly just is not enough, for God is love, and we must love our neighbor as ourselves; to give every one his due is not sufficient, we must act upon those same principles of grace which reign in the heart of God. The promises of establishment and prosperity are not to rude Nabals, nor to stingy Labans, but to bountiful souls who have proved their fitness to be stewards of the Lord by dealing graciously with their substance.

March 23

Plautus would have gossipers and their listeners alike punished by hanging, the one by the tongue the other by the ears. We should soon be short of timber for the gallows if this clever sentence were carried out, but there is no need that any one of us should earn the right to swing among their company. If telephones and microphones are carried much further, we shall have enough of hearing and over-hearing, and it will be wise for us to cultivate deafness when others are chattering. "Study to be quiet."

March 24

Few prodigals will ever seek their father's house till they are half-starved, and for their best interests it is far better for them to be empty and faint than to be full and stout-hearted. If hunger brings us to our knees, it is more useful to us than feasting; a famine in the land and a famine in the heart may be our heavenly Father's messengers to fetch us home to himself.

March 25

Climbing up the olive terraces and steep mountain sides at Mentone, we find it needful to look at every footstep lest our feeble feet should cause us to fall; and when we ascend a hill which is new to us, we have to take our bearings pretty frequently lest we should miss our course. No man can go to heaven blindly. The eye of faith which looks to Christ will be needed all the way, and he who closes it will soon be tripped up by one stumbling block or another.

March 26

Servants of Jesus Christ, never be discouraged when you are opposed, but when things run counter to your wishes expect that the Lord has provided some better thing for you. He is driving you away from shallow waters and bringing you into deeper seas, where your nets shall bring you larger draughts. Like the Israelites, you shall find that your enemies shall be bread for you instead you shall eat them. "Be strong, fear not."

March 27

Strings are wonderful things when a master musician plays upon them—they seem to grow sympathetic and incorporated with the minstrel, as if his very soul were imparted to them and thrilled through them. Only when a thoroughly enraptured heart speaks in the instrument can music be acceptable to God; as mere musical sound the Lord can have no pleasure therein: he is only pleased with the thought and feeling which are thus expressed. This licensed David's harp, but it would silence many an organ.

March 28

God, like a wise father, trains us prudently, and as we are able to bear it, he makes our service and our suffering more and more arduous. As boys rejoice to be treated like men, so will we rejoice in our greater tribulations, for here is man's work for us, and by God's help we will not flinch from doing it. "Conduct yourselves like men; be strong."

March 29

There was but one crack in the lantern, and the wind has found it out and blown out the candle. How great a mischief one unguarded point of character may cause us! One spark blew up the magazine and shook the whole country for miles around. One leak sank the vessel and drowned all on board. One wound may kill the body, one sin destroys the soul. "Search me, O Lord"; yet would I rather cry, "Save me, O Lord."

March 30

In the ancient times a box on the ear given by a master to a slave meant liberty; little would the freed man care how hard was the blow. By a stroke from the sword the warrior was knighted by his monarch—small matter was it to the new-made knight if the royal hand was heavy. When the Lord intends to lift his servants into a higher stage of spiritual life he frequently sends them a severe trial.

March 31

The atoning work of Jesus is the great gun of our artillery. The cross is the mighty battering-ram which is used to break in pieces the brazen gates of human prejudices and the iron bars of obstinacy. Christ coming to be our Judge alarms, but Christ the Man of Sorrows subdues. The crown of thorns has a royal power in it to compel a willing allegiance, the scepter of reed breaks hearts better than a rod of iron, and the robe of mockery commands more love than Caesar's imperial purple.

April 1

A Christian making money fast is like a man caught in a cloud of dust: it will fill his eyes if he be not careful. A Christian full of worldly care is in the same condition, and had need look to it, lest he be choked with earth. Afflictions might almost be prayed for, if we never had them, even as in long stretches of fair weather, men beg for rain to lay the dust. An April shower, though it may seem to spoil a day, may be a great blessing.

April 2

The martyrs' blood is the purple vesture of the church of Christ: the trials and persecutions of believers are her crown of thorns. Think of the rage of persecution in every land, and you will see how the emblem of Christ's kingdom is a crown of thorns. A crown, and yet thorns; thorns, but still a crown. This also is the coat of arms of every soldier of the cross.

April 3

Perhaps the brightest weather is just when the rain has ceased, when the wind chases away the clouds, and the sun peers forth from its chambers to gladden the earth with its smiles. Thus is it with the Christian's exercised heart. Sorrow does not last forever; after the pelting rain of adversity comes ever and soon the "clear shining." Tried believer, consider this. After all your afflictions there remains a rest for the people of God.

April 4

I saw a garden in spring so sprinkled with anemones of every hue that it made me dream that a rainbow had been stolen from the skies and spread upon the ground. And why not? Why should not some glimmerings of heaven linger among us still? We are on the way there, may we not expect foretastes of it? Should not our Sabbaths be foreshadowings of the eternal Sabbath, and our communion seasons pledges and forecasts of the fellowship of the skies?

April 5

It is said that if a condemned criminal in Madagascar can but see the Queen, his life is sure to be spared, such is the tenderness of the monarch's heart. It is still more sure that if a sinner will but look at King Jesus he shall live. Who would refuse to look when life comes thereby? Dear reader, look at Jesus! Look now, before you close this book.

April 6

Do you find yourselves forgetful of Jesus? It is the incessant turmoil of the world, the constant attraction of earthly things, which takes away the soul from Christ. While memory too well preserves a poisonous weed, it suffers the Rose of Sharon to wither. Let us charge ourselves to bind an unfading forget-me-not about our hearts in honor of our heavenly Bridegroom, and whatever else we let slip let us ever remember Him. "Lord, remember me,"

April 7

Light is the cause of beauty. Nothing of beauty is left when light is gone. Without light no radiance flashes from the sapphire, no peaceful ray proceeds from the pearl; and thus all the loveliness of the perfected above and of the redeemed below comes from Jesus. As planets, they reflect the light of the Sun of Righteousness. The whole redeemed church, like the moon, shines with a borrowed radiance— the glory of the Lord Jesus Christ.

April 8

As the earth drinks in the rain, as the sea receives the streams, as the night accepts light from the stars, so we, giving nothing, partake freely of the grace of God. The saints are not by nature wells or streams, but they are cisterns into which the living water flows. They are empty vessels into which the Lord pours his salvation. Lord, fill my soul till it runs over with praise!

April 9

Come in, O strong and deep love of Jesus, like the sea at flood-tide, cover all my powers, drown all my sins, sweep away all my cares, lift up my earth-bound soul, and float it right up to my Lord's feet, and there let me lie, a poor broken shell, washed up by his love, having no virtue or value, and only venturing to whisper to him that, if he will put his ear to me, he will hear within faint echoes of the vast waves of his own love which have brought me where it is my delight to lie, even at his feet forever.

April 10

Let us never boast ourselves of tomorrow, for we know not what a day may bring. The promises of the new morning are not often fulfilled; clouds gather, and the sun which rose in splendor sets in showers. We make our nest as downy as it can be, and then say, "Soul, take thine ease: thy mountain standeth firm, thou shalt never be moved." But, ah, how soon the mountain shakes, the nest is filled with thorns, and the joy vanishes!

April 11

Much ignorance of Jesus may remain in hearts which yet feel the power of his blood. We must not hastily condemn men for lack of knowledge, for we know very little ourselves. Where we perceive a true faith in Jesus we need not question the fact of salvation, however scanty the learning. The Holy Spirit makes men repentant long before he makes them divines; and he who believes what he knows, shall soon know more clearly what he believes.

April 12

Our God has not left us at any time. We have had dark nights, but the star of love has shone forth amid the blackness; we have been in stern conflicts, but over our head he has held aloft the shield of our defense. We have gone through many trials, but never to our detriment, always to our advantage; and our conclusion from our past experience is that he who has been with us in six troubles will not forsake us in the seventh. "Trust in him at all times."

April 13

Faith prospers most when all things are against her; trials are her trainers, and lightnings are her illuminators. When calmness reigns on the sea the ship makes no headway; for on a slumbering ocean the keel sleeps too. Let the winds rush howling forth, and let the waters lift up themselves, and, though the vessel's deck may be washed with waves, and her mast may creak under the pressure of the swelling sail, it is then that she speeds towards her desired haven.

April 14

Here, my best joys bear "mortal" on their brow, my fair bowers fade, my dainty cups are drained to dregs, my sweetest birds fall before death's arrows, my pleasant days are shadowed into nights, and the flood tides of my bliss subside into ebbs of sorrow; but in heaven everything is immortal, the harp abides unrusted, the crown unwithered, the eye undimmed, the voice unfaltering, the heart unwavering, and the entire being is bathed in infinite delight.

April 15

Behold, at this hour our moral history is being preserved for eternity. Processes are at work which will perpetuate our every act, and word, and thought. Not alone the last page, but every line and letter of our actual history is being stereotyped for the world's perusal in the day which shall reveal the secrets of men. We are not writing upon the water, but carving upon imperishable material. The chapters of our history are "graven with an iron pen and lead in the rock forever."

April 16

We grow, we wax mighty, we prevail by private prayer. That we may be strong to labor, tender to sympathize, and wise to direct, let us pray. If study makes men of us, prayer will make saints of us. Our sacred furnishing for a holy life can only be found in the arsenal of supplication, and after we have entered upon our consecrated warfare, prayer alone can keep our armor bright.

April 17

Truth runs in two parallel lines, if not in three or more; and when the Holy Spirit sets before us one line he wisely points out to us the other. The truth of divine sovereignty is qualified by human responsibility, and the teaching of abounding grace is seasoned by the remembrance of unflinching justice. Scripture gives us, as it were, the acid and the alkali, the rock and the oil which flows from it, the sword which cuts, and the balm which heals. Accept both.

April 18

Death's black extinguisher must soon put out your candle. Oh! how sweet to have sunlight when the candle is gone! The dark flood must soon roll between you and all you have on earth; see to it that you have treasure in heaven. Wed your heart to him who will never leave you; trust your self with him who will go with you through the torrent of death, land you safely on the celestial shore, and make you sit with him in the heavenly places forever.

April 19

Virtues without faith are whitewashed sins. Unbelief nullifies everything. It is the fly in the ointment; the poison in the pot. Without faith—with all the virtues of purity, with all the benevolence of philanthropy, with all the kindness of sympathy, with all the talent of genius, and with all the bravery of patriotism, a man has no title to divine acceptance; for "without faith it is impossible to please God."

April 20

For many weeks no land was seen nor a single vessel sighted, but the captain was well skilled in navigation, and the good ship held on her way. A fog came on, and the boat lay still. According to the reckoning they were near port; and when the fog lifted, and the crew saw the harbor lights right ahead, they gave three hearty cheers for the captain. We, too, are sailing by faith, with Jesus at the helm. What will our shouts be when we shall see heaven right ahead, and shall not have to change our course half a point!

April 21

See that creeping caterpillar, how contemptible its appearance! It is the beginning of a thing. Mark that insect with gorgeous wings, playing in the sunbeams, sipping at the flower-bells, full of happiness and life; that is the end thereof. That caterpillar is you until you are wrapped up in the chrysalis of death; but when Christ shall appear you shall be like him, for you shall see him as he is.

April 22

Happy are they who die in the Lord; they rest from their labors, and their works follow them. The quiet repose of their bodies shall never be broken until God shall arouse them to give them their full reward. Guarded by angel watchers, curtained by eternal mysteries, they sleep on, the inheritors of glory, till the fullness of time shall bring the fullness of redemption. What an awaking shall be theirs!

April 23

The sensitive plant, as soon as it is touched, begins to fold up its leaves. Touch it again and the little branches droop, until at last it stands like the bare poles of a vessel; all its sail of leaf is furled, and it seems as if it would, if it could, shrink into nothing to avoid your hand. So should we be in this world, sensitive to the touch of sin, grieved by the approach of evil.

April 24

There is a spot in Mentone called the Primrose Valley;not because there are no other plants there, but because in the season it teems with that favorite flower. The Christian is said to live the life of faith, not because he is destitute of other graces, for he wears them all, but because this divine virtue is for many reasons the most abundant in him. So, also, God is said to be love, though he is also powerful and just, because love abounds in him, and is most conspicuous in all his dealings.

April 25

Christ purifies those whom he pardons. The cross gives sanctity as well as safety. Think not to put asunder what God has joined together, for our personal holiness is the practical object of our Lord's perfect sacrifice he: "gave himself for us, that he might redeem us from all iniquity, and purify unto himself a peculiar people, zealous of good works."

April 26

In the church of Rome they have certain orders of men and women who wholly give themselves to benevolent, charitable, or superstitious works, and who come to be specially considered as religious devotees. We have never admired these fraternities and sisterhoods; but we must do; more than they. Body, soul, and spirit must be entirely dedicated to Jesus. "What do ye more than others?"

April 27

Wrestling prayer is a great benefit to the Christian. As the runner gains strength for the race by daily exercise, so for the great race of life we acquire energy by the hallowed training of persistent prayer. Prayer plumes the wings of God's young eaglets, that they may learn to mount above the clouds. Prayer girds the loins of God's warriors, and sends them forth to combat with their sinews braced and their muscles firm.

April 28

As an eminent merchant was dying, he exclaimed, "The blood of Christ is all to me. I hang upon the atonement." Would it bear his weight? He found it fully able to do so for he died in an ecstasy of joy. This should not be surprising, for this same Christ is the axle of the wheel of nature, the stone which bears up all things. Lean all your weight on him, for his infinite grace will sustain millions upon millions of sinners.

April 29

When sin conquered the realm of manhood it slew all the minstrels except those of the race of hope. For humanity, amid all its sorrows and sins, hope sings on. To believers in Jesus there remains a royal race of bards, for we have a hope of glory, a lively hope, a hope eternal and divine. Because our hope abides our praise continues—"I will hope continually, and will yet praise thee more and more."

April 30

Let those who love the Lord Jesus Christ be ashamed to play the coward, and come out and own their glorious Captain. Should not the soldier wear his red coat? Should he hide his regimentals? You would despise such a man. Is Christ then to be the leader of a troop of cowards? What are you ashamed of? Be ashamed of being ashamed, if you are ashamed of Christ.

May 1

In Jesus I find not only fragrance, but a bed of spices; not one blossom, but all manner of sweet flowers. He is to me my rose and my lily, my heartsease, and my cluster of camphire. When he is with me it is May all the year round, and my soul goes forth to wash her happy face in the morning dew of his grace, and to solace herself with the singing Precious Lord Jesus, let me in every deed know the blessedness which dwells in abiding, Unbroken fellowship with thee.

May 2

It is much to be desired that all day long, in every hobby, in every recreation, and even in every tribulation, the soul should spontaneously pour forth praise, even as birds sing, and flowers perfume the air, and sunbeams cheer the earth. We would be incarnate psalmody, praise enshrined in flesh and blood. From this delightful duty we would desire no cessation and ask no pause. "Praise waiteth for thee, O God, in Zion."

May 3

Not all the music blown from sweet instruments, or drawn from living strings can yield such melody as this sweet promise, "I will be their God." Here is a deep sea of bliss, a shoreless ocean of delight: come, bathe your spirit in it. Swim an age, and you will find no shore; dive throughout eternity, and you will find no bottom. If this does not make your eyes sparkle, and your heart beat high with bliss, then assuredly your soul is not in a healthy state.

May 4

"God saw the light, that it was good." Spiritual light has many beams and prismatic colors, but whether they be knowledge, joy, holiness, or life, all are divinely good. If the light received be thus good, what must the essential light be, and how glorious must be the place where he reveals Himself, and banishes every cloud. O Lord, since light is so good, give us more of it, and more of Yourself, the true light.

May 5

Let not your zeal evaporate in a mere mist of pious talk, let it flow in streams of practical usefulness. Love the brethren of him who loved you. If there be a Mephibosheth anywhere who is lame or halt, help him for that Jonathan's sake whose love to you surpassed the love of women. If there be a poor tried believer, weep with him, and bear his cross for the sake of him who wept for you, and carried the painful burden of your sins.

May 6

If you have a touch of despondency in your nature take care to subdue it to the Lord's praise. You are the man to sing those "grave, sweet melodies" which are the pearls of song. A little pensiveness is good flavoring for joy. The muse is at her best when she is pleasingly melancholy. Praise God after your own manner. Larks must sing though they are not nightingales, nor must the sparrow refuse to chirp because he cannot emulate the finch.

May 7

"There is no love among Christians," cries the man who is destitute of true charity. "Zeal has vanished," exclaims the idle talker. "O for more consistency," groans the hypocrite. "We want more vital godliness," protests the false pretender. As, in the legend, the wolf preached against sheep-stealing, so very many hunt down those sins in others which they gladly shelter in themselves.

May 8

Paul, when grown old, sitting gray-haired, shivering in a dungeon in Rome, could say with greater emphasis than we can—"I know whom I have believed," for each experience had been like the climbing of a hill, each trial had been like ascending another summit, and his death seemed like gaining the top of the mountain, from which he could see the whole of the faithfulness and love of the Lord to whom he had committed his soul.

May 9

When slips of flowers are first put into the ground they want more water than they will require afterwards. When they have sent out more roots, and these roots have produced abundant fibers to search through the soil for moisture, they will not require much of the gardener's care, but just now they must have it, or die; therefore, I say, let the feeble, the weak, the young beginners in grace be watered most anxiously and lovingly by all who seek their good.

May 10

The first stone in the breastplate of the High Priest was a sardius or ruby.

> The sardius stone is shining red
> Deep with the hue of blood o'erspread;
> In this our faith may fitly see
> Th' atonement's matchless mystery.

We see no preciousness in our Lord Jesus till we have known the power of his atoning blood. Neither emerald nor sapphire can delight us till we have first gazed on the ruby.

May 11

Lack of confidence is the great hindrance in learning to swim. Struggle, and you will sink; be quiet, and the stream sustains you. The hard point is to remove your foot from the bottom and commit yourself to the water. He who casts himself upon the upbearing power of the liquid will soon master the art of swimming, but there must be no reserve. So is it with faith: there must be no visible support, no reliance upon self. Take off hand and foot from self-confidence, and cast yourself alone on Jesus, and you are saved.

May 12

Truth is as the clusters of the vine which need treading in the wine vat before they yield their generous juice. We must cast the doctrines of Scripture into the wine press of meditation and tread them with the joyful feet of holy thought, or their refreshing essence will be wasted. "Meditate on these things, give thyself wholly to them."

May 13

The eclipse of your faith, the darkness of your mind, the fainting of your hope, all these things are but part of God's method of making you ripe for heaven. There are "precious things put forth by the moon" needing night to perfect them; and perhaps some parts of your character are such fruits. Bear the gloom and damp patiently, for you will soon reach the land of which it is written, "There shall be no night there."

May 14

Most of us are mere beginners in spiritual education; for we have scarcely learned our letters as yet. An old divine says, "He that has been in heaven but five minutes knows more than the general assembly of divines on earth." Still as there is nothing in all the books of the Bodleian library but what may be expressed by the letters of the alphabet, so he who knows Jesus as Alpha and Omega knows the essence of all heavenly wisdom.

May 15

If I look at Peter, I admire his courage; if I look at Paul, I wonder at his devotedness; if I look at John, I marvel at his love; but when I behold the Savior, I am not so much attracted by any one particular virtue as by the singular combination of the whole. Each saint wears a jewel, but on the breast of our High Priest we see all the gems at once.

May 16

We are not to retain the precious grains of truth as the Egyptian mummy held the wheat for ages, without giving it an opportunity to grow; we must sow it and water it. Why does the Lord send down the rain upon the thirsty earth and give the genial sunshine? Is it not that these may all help the earth to yield food for man? Even so the Lord visits and refreshes our souls that we may use our renewed strength in the promotion of his glory.

May 17

As often as we read a new title of the Redeemer let us appropriate him as ours under that name. The shepherd's staff, the captain's sword, the priest's mitre, the prince's scepter, the prophet's mantle, are all ours, since Christ is ours. Jesus has no dignity which he will not employ for our exaltation, and no prerogative which he will not exercise for our defense. His fullness of godhead and perfection of manhood are our inexhaustible treasure-house.

May 18

The sea is made of drops and the rocks are composed of grains. The sea which divides thy heart from Christ may be filled with the drops of thy little sins, and the rock which has nearly wrecked the ship of your soul may have been built up by the daily working of the coral insects of your unnoticed faults. If you would live with Christ, and walk with Christ, and have fellowship with Christ, take heed of the "little foxes that spoil the vines."

May 19

Where the best wine is produced the vines are very sharply trimmed, and are cut down almost to the root. Where they grow upon trellises there is a gain to the landscape, but a loss in the flavor of the wines. Mostly the Lord has his highest glory from the most afflicted saints, and though prosperity may give the Christian a more showy figure among men, it often lessens the inward savor of his graces.

May 20

We live upon Christ daily, but in times of great trial we find him to be our munitions of war as well as our manna. Brave men not long ago baffled thousands by fighting behind a rampart of biscuit boxes and corn bags, and by God's grace we will imitate them. Those precious gospel truths which are our heavenly bread shall also be our bulwark. Come on, ye Zulus of free thought or superstition; with Christ between us and you we defy your rage!

May 21

Just now we saw two eagles high above us, but they appeared to be very insignificant birds; their distance so dwarfed them to our sight that we fancied they were crows. Thus is the dread day of judgment lightly esteemed by men because it seems to be far off. Oh that men would know that it draws near! "The Judge stands at the door."

May 22

God's promises are to the Christian as the granaries which Joseph filled in preparation for the years of famine, and he resorts to them without fear of their exhaustion. Blessed is he who can take the five barley loaves and fishes of promise and break them till his five thousand necessities are all supplied, and he is able to gather up twelve baskets full of fragments. God's promises are better than man's performances; one word of God is worth more than the whole world.

May 23

We sat for half-an-hour in a calf's shed the other day, quite grateful for the shelter from the driving rain, yet at no other time would we have entered such a dirty place. Discontented persons need a course of the bread of adversity and the water of affliction to cure them of the wretched habit of murmuring. Even things which we loathed before, we learn to prize when in troubling circumstances.

May 24

It is very likely that neither ministers nor their sermons are perfect—the best garden may have a few weeds in it, the cleanest corn may have some chaff—but criticizers carp at anything or nothing and find fault for the sake of showing off their deep knowledge. Sooner than let their tongues have a holiday, they would complain that the grass is not a nice shade of blue, and declare that the sky would have been more beautiful if it had been whitewashed.

May 25

Dream not that a long period intervenes between the instant of death and the eternity of glory. When the eyes close on earth they open in heaven. The horses of fire are not an instant on the road. Then, O child of God, what is there for you to fear in death, seeing that through the death of your Lord its curse and sting are destroyed? And now it is but a Jacob's ladder, whose foot is in the dark grave, but whose topmost round reaches to glory everlasting.

May 26

Our soul is even as the clusters of the vine; which belong alone to the owner of the vineyard. Great Lord, let my every cluster and grape be gathered by you alone. Cast me into the wine vat of your service, and let my whole soul flow forth for you; let the ruddy juice burst forth on the right hand and on the left, and when the first rich liquor of my youth is gone, then even to the utmost lees let me be pressed till the last drop of the living juice shall have flowed forth for you alone.

May 27

Boasting is a sure sign of failure; even Goliath, the giant, had hardly finished boasting before his proud forehead lay prone in the dust. Chase pride from your soul, for it is foolish, and the mother of folly; it is a noxious insect which will corrupt whatever it lights upon, gaudy though its wings may be. Pride betrays the emptiness of its owner. The jewel of grace has a humble jewelry box. Gilded wood will float, but solid gold will sink.

May 28

Surrounded by a wealth of many-colored flowers which dazzled and delighted us, we were told of a fellow-traveler who had no sense of color, and could not detect even the boldest differences of hue. How we pitied him! Yet, reader, he is far more to be grieved over who cannot perceive the charms of true religion, the perfections of the Lord Jesus. He is stone-blind who does not admire the Rose of Sharon, the Lily of the valleys.

May 29

Our afflictions are like weights, and have a tendency to drag us to the dust, but there is a way of arranging weights by means of wheels and pulleys, so that they will even lift us up. Grace, by its matchless art, has often turned the heaviest of our trials into occasions for heavenly joy. "We glory in tribulations also."

May 30

Loving jealousy of our Lord's honor makes us tremble when we speak of him. An earnest admirer of art in pointing with his walking-stick to the beauties of a famous picture pushed his cane through the canvas and ruined it; and it is possible that in our enthusiasm to point out the beauties and perfections of the life and death of our Lord, we may spoil it all. Earnest therefore is our prayer—"Lord, open thou my lips; and my mouth shall show forth thy praise."

May 31

See how a baby trusts its mother; even so must we trust in Jesus. See how the spider drops from the ceiling and rises again by an invisible thread, so must we hang by faith upon what Christ has done, and rise to heaven thereby. As the mariner relies on his compass, whose mystery he cannot solve, and the voyager in a balloon depends upon a gas which he cannot see, so must we trust in him whom having not seen we love.

June 1

See how the little children weave garlands and chaplets, and are as happy as the merry birds, while arrayed in collars and girdles made of the flowers of the field. Will they be any wiser when only diamonds and gold will serve their turn? Is not a simple taste which loves nature the best after all? So, too, in reading the Scriptures, it is better to revel in its plain promises and precious privileges than to pine for erudite criticisms and theological disputations.

June 2

If I find myself growing in God's garden, though I be the tiniest plant in all the bed, yet it is such a mercy to be in the garden at all—I, who was a wild, rank weed, out in the wilderness before—that I will not doubt but what He will water me when I need it, and that He will tend and care for me till I shall come to perfection. Has he not said of every plant in his garden, "I will water it every moment"?

June 3

Nothing is made in vain. Though no lip of man is moistened by the brook in the lone valley, yet other creatures need refreshment, and these quench their thirst at the stream. Is this nothing? Must everything exist for man, or else be wasted? God does not think so. What but our pride and selfishness could have suggested such a notion? It is not true that flowers which blush unseen of human eye are wasting their sweetness, for the bee finds them out, and other winged wanderers live on their luscious juices.

June 4

He who would serve God must begin by loving him, for a grateful, loving heart is the spring of obedience. We must offer the salt of gratitude with the sacrifice of service. Our faces should shine with the joyfulness of praise. As soldiers march to music, so while we walk in the paths of righteousness we should keep step to the notes of thanksgiving. Larks sing as they mount, and so should we magnify the Lord for his mercies while we are winging our way to heaven.

June 5

Darkness is more fit for beasts than for men; and those men are most brutish who love darkness rather than light. When the darkness of ignorance broods over a nation, then all sorts of superstitions, cruelties, and vices abound; the gospel, like the sunrise, soon delivers a nation from the open ravages of these monsters, and they seek more pleasing abodes. Spread well the gospel light if you would keep the Roman wolf from our folds.

June 6

If we are walking, we go from strength to weakness. We start fresh and in good order for our journey, but by-and-by the road is rough, and the sun is hot, and we sit down by the wayside to rest a while. Painfully we rise and pursue our way, with heavier footsteps. But Christian pilgrims, having obtained fresh supplies of grace, are as vigorous after years of toilsome travel as when they first turned their faces Zionward. "They shall walk, and not faint."

June 7

Christian, you may rejoice in your safety in Christ; but you must not dream that you are safe from attack. You are like a stream from Lebanon, to be dashed down many a cascade, to be broken over many a rough rock, to be hindered by many a huge stone, to be impeded by many a fallen tree; but you are to dash forward with the irresistible force of God, sweeping everything before you, till you reach the ocean of eternal joy. We are cast down, but not forsaken."

June 8

A prince who had revolted from his allegiance to Rome sent presents to the Roman general, but these were returned with the warning that his gifts could not be accepted by the Roman State so long as he remained in rebellion. Neither will the Lord accept the services of men whose hearts are far from him. Would you receive a bouquet of flowers from a servant who refused to do your bidding? Would you not bid her first to attend to her work? So must you first love God, before your religious observances can be pleasing to him.

June 9

Have I been making a fair show in the flesh without having a corresponding inner life? Let me reflect that in flourishing plants growth takes place upwards and downwards at the same time. It may be that I am flowering with conspicuous zeal, like a scarlet poppy among corn; but am I rooted in sincere fidelity and love to Jesus? If not, my profession will soon die away for want of root.

June 10

Oh, it charms me to think that when we let loose the truth in the power of the Spirit we never know where it will fly. A child takes one of those little downy seeds which has its own parachute to uplift it from the ground: the little one blows it into the air, but who knows where that downy seed shall settle, and in whose garden it shall grow? That it will live and grow is certain. Such is truth, even from the mouths of babes.

June 11

What was sung of Italy may yet more truly be said of Palestine:—
"Thy very weeds are beautiful, thy waste
More rich than other climes' fertility."
Thy land, O Emmanuel, once the glory of all lands, is
"Even in her ruin graced
With an immaculate charm which cannot be defaced."
When shall the land again receive the favored nation, and Jesus
be its King? Let us heartily pray for the Jewish nation.

June 12

Do not the thorns of the rose protect it from the assaults of
snails and grubs, which else might eat out its very heart? Are
they not as a phalanx around the ruddy beauty? Would you
have the flower without it? Then it is probable that you would
soon be without the flower. The ruggedness of honesty and the
suspicion of prudence may make the virtuous seem somewhat
unapproachable; but in this wicked world these guards are very
needful.

June 13

When a key has often turned in the lock it goes more and more
easily; so, praying fits for praying, and meditation leads on to
meditation. Things difficult to beginners grow delightful after a
little practice. Therefore do not cease from a duty because you
find it hard, for this is just a proof of how much you need to
perform it. Press on till you get into the swing of holy habit,
and by gracious assistance are able to sing, "Or ever I was aware,
my soul made me like the chariots of Amminadib."

June 14

Every grace should be practiced in its season. It would be idle to make fires in summer, or to deck the grate with ornaments in winter. Patience is out of place while we enjoy pleasure, and courage is not needed when enemies are absent. Some men's virtues are always out of town when they are called upon: be it ours to bring forth our fruit in its season.

June 15

Cowper says of a certain vine, when it climbs the ash or beech, that "She does a mischief while she lends a grace." It is to be feared that this is the net result of sending our children to receive education upon the Continent, and of much that is thought to be culture in our own country. That which renders us unfaithful to the truth is an evil to be dreaded, however much it may cause us to be esteemed among men. Piety is better than polish, and goodness than gentility.

June 16

As the sun first shines on the mountain tops, gilds them with its light, and thus presents one of the most charming sights to the traveler's eye, so is it delightful to mark the glow of the Spirit's light in the saint who has risen high in spiritual stature. Like a snow-capped mountain he reflects the beams of the Sun of righteousness, and bears the sheen of his bursting radiance high aloft for all to see; and, seeing it, to glorify the great Father of lights.

June 17

Certain meats are pleasant in the eating but leave an ill flavor in the mouth, whereas many bitter substances leave an agreeable taste behind. Carnal joys are followed by after sorrows, but holy duties yield a subsequent content. The sinner never leaves his sports with such a merry heart as we bring with us from the throne of grace. After a sorrowful prayer Hannah's spirit was sad no more. Though repentance be bitter, it yields a sweet peace, and the most mournful duty creates the most intense delight.

June 18

When a man becomes nothing in his own estimation, then Jesus Christ becomes everything to him, and not till then. Self is an effectual darkener of the windows of the soul. How can men see the gospel while they see so much of themselves? With such a noble righteousness of their own to deck themselves with, is it likely that they will buy of Christ the fine linen which is the righteousness of saints?

June 19

When the good shepherd found the lost sheep he did not drive or even lead it back. It was too weary and worn to reach the fold, and so he carried it. It was so with me, I had not a step to go, I looked to the Great Shepherd and I was peacefully in his fold without further effort.

"Love on its shoulders joyfully did lay
Me, weary with the greatness of my way."

Look, dear seeking reader, and it shall be so with you.

June 20

Although no man can have too much religion, there are some who are burnt black with bigoted zeal for their favorite fragment of truth, or are charred to a cinder with the vainglorious ostentation of those religious performances which suit their humor. The assumed appearance of superior sanctity frequently accompanies a total absence of vital godliness. The saint in public may be a devil in private, dealing in flour by day and in soot by night.

June 21

I passed under a camphor tree and gathered a few of its leaves and found them full of camphor; indeed, the whole of the tree was saturated with it. So should the grace of God show itself in the whole life of the believer. As the inevitable outflow of his renewed nature his most commonplace acts and words should be gracious. Little things best reveal character, for in them a man is less upon his guard. Let even the leaves of your words partake of the grace which dwells in you.

June 22

Those who are soaked in worldly pleasures are incompetent to judge of the sweetness of the heavenly life. If they can relish the grapes of Gomorrha, they are not likely to prize the clusters of Eshcol. A dog is no judge of jewelery; throw him a bone, and he is better pleased than if you gave him the crown jewels. When men sneer at us for our godliness we need not be disturbed by it; we should the rather pity them because of their loss of those noble faculties which would teach them better.

June 23

The faintest movement of the pulse proves that life still remains in a drowning man, and though prayer be weak, feeble, fragmentary, yet if the soul prays at all, it lives unto God. Have hope, brother, as long as you can pray, for none who pray believingly, in the name of Jesus, can ever be cast into hell. He whom faith in Jesus has taught to cry to God shall never hear him say, "Depart, ye cursed;" for has not the Lord said, "Whosoever shall call upon the name of the Lord shall be saved"?

June 24

As when on a sultry day the traveler strips off his garments, and plunges into the cool, refreshing brook, and rises from it invigorated to pursue his way, so when a spirit has learned, either in prayer or in praise, really to draw near to God, it bathes itself in the brooks of heaven (streams branching from the river of the water of life), and goes on its way renewed with heavenly strength.

June 25

You will best know Christ by following in his footsteps. Poverty will reveal him who for our sakes became poor; sickness will show him whose visage was more marred than any man's; shame will teach you his shame, and suffering will reveal to you his suffering; yea, even death itself, which shall uncover the foundations of your faith, shall give you conformity to his death that you may have part in his resurrection.

June 26

It is marvelous how thin the wire may be which carries the electric charge. We need a cable to carry a message across the sea, but that is for the protection of the wire; the wire itself, which actually carries the message, is a slender thing. So even a little faith in Christ links us with God, and the life of God comes to us thereby. The connecting medium may be a mere spider's thread of trembling faith; but, if it runs all the way from the heart of Christ to our heart, divine grace can and will flow through it.

June 27

Christian men should know that there are many false lights shown along the shores of life, and, therefore, the true light is greatly needed. The wreckers of Satan are always abroad, tempting the ungodly to sin under the name of pleasure. They hoist the wrong light; be it ours to put up the true light upon every dangerous rock, to point out every sin, and tell what it leads to, that so we may be clear of the blood of all men, shining as lights in the world.

June 28

You cannot grow in grace to any high degree while you remain rooted to the world. Decision for Christ may be a thorny path, but it is the highway of safety; and though the separated life may cost you many pangs, yet it is a happy life after all. No joy can excel that of the man who earns the enmity of the world by his love to the Savior. Jesus reveals himself so graciously, and gives such sweet refreshment, that the soldier of the cross feels more of calm and peace in his daily strife than others in their carnal ease.

June 29

Pray about everything, little as well as great, joyous as well as sad. "In everything by prayer and supplication with thanksgiving let your requests be made known unto God." That evil which you pray over will lose its sting, and the good which is mentioned at the throne of grace will have its sweetness sanctified. Prayer will make tribulation endurable, even if it does not transform it into rejoicing. A trouble prayed over is a dead lion with honey in the carcass.

June 30

Praise the Lord for the sun of joy when it rises, and for the evening of sorrow as it falls. There is beauty both in sunrise and in sunset; sing of it and glorify the Lord. Like the nightingale, pour forth happy notes at midnight. Believe that the night of weeping is as useful as the morning of joy. The dews of grace fall heavily in the night of sorrow. The stars of promise shine forth conspicuously amid the darkness of grief. "We glory in tribulations also."

July 1

There was never such a child of perdition as Judas. Never one sank in the depths of divine wrath with so huge a millstone about his neck as that man, who had lived so close to our Lord. What a warning is this to all who make an open profession and enjoy great privileges! The same sun ripens the corn and the hemlock: a man may be matured in crime by the same external processes which perfect others in holiness.

July 2

Huber, the great naturalist, tells us, that if a single wasp discovers a deposit of honey or other food, he will return to his nest and impart the good news to his companions, who will sally forth in great numbers to partake of the fare which has been discovered for them. Shall we who have found honey in the rock Christ Jesus be less considerate of our fellow men than wasps are of their fellow insects?

July 3

Rich men contribute a guinea, and modestly say, "Put it down as the widow's mite." My dear sir, it was in the plural, "two mites." Make it two guineas, so as to be accurate in number, at any rate. Then remember that she gave "all her living," and you defraud her if you call your donation by her name, and do not give a hundredth part of your substance. If minute subscribers out of magnificent incomes would truly imitate the widow what a revenue would pour in!

July 4

If those who spend so many hours in idle company, light reading, and useless pastimes could learn wisdom, they would find more profitable society in communion with heaven, and more interesting occupation in holy meditation than in the vanities which now ensnare them. What man would choose to consort with beggars if he might enjoy the society of princes? Who would wish to roll in the mire when he might lie in beds of spices?

July 5

School boards have many subjects to teach, but they need not appoint a department for instruction in crying, for that is natural to all children. Even so, a spiritual cry is the voice of the newborn nature expressing conscious need. "How shall I pray?" says one. Pour out your heart. Turn the vessel upside down, and let it run out to the last dreg, as best it can: this is prayer. May the Holy Spirit help you in it. "This poor man cried and the Lord heard him."

July 6

Graces unexercised are as sweet perfumes slumbering in the cups of the flowers. The wisdom of the great Husbandman overrules diverse and opposite causes to produce the one desired result of shedding abroad the fragrance which grace gives us. The winds of affliction and the sun of joy alike draw forth grateful odors from the fair flowers: of the garden of the heart, such as faith, love, patience, hope, resignation, joy, and the like.

July 7

When prayer is heard in our feebleness, and answered in the power of God, we are strengthened in the habit of prayer and confirmed in the resolve to make ceaseless intercession. "Because he hath inclined his ear unto me, therefore will I call upon him as long as I live." We should not thank a beggar who informed us that because we had granted his request he would never cease to beg of us, and yet it is most acceptable to God that his petitioners should resolve to beg as long as they breathe.

July 8

Home is especially a woman's sphere. There she reigns as queen; let her throne be established in love. Around the hearth and at the table, in the sweets of domestic relationship and quiet friendship, a woman will do more for the glory of the Lord Jesus Christ than by climbing into a pulpit. In the cases of men also, many who long to flash in public had better by far shine at home.

July 9

One longs to see the popular idea of holiness once for all dissociated from anything unreal and unpractical, and yoked with the common virtues of everyday life. The smashing up of the whole caravan of sanctified waxworks, which, in years gone by, have attracted ignorant admiration, would be a special benefit to our race; and the exhibition of real, household, common-sense religion in its most vigorous form would be, under God, one of the greatest blessings which our age could receive. "Show piety at home."

July 10

Let not Jesus be a shadow to you, or your religion will be unsubstantial; let him not be a name to you, or your religion will be nominal; let him not be a myth of history, or your religion will be mere fancy. Regard him as more than a teacher, or you will fail to appreciate the merit of his blood; let him be all in all to you, or you will miss some of his perfections. Set him on a glorious high throne, or you will never lead a glorious life.

July 11

Did you ever see a poor, shivering, miserable beggar in the street starving for want of food, and yet curious about the exact details of the imperial revenues for the current quarter of the year! What business can that be of his? Is it not his first business to win a morsel of bread? And should it not be your first concern as a man, that you should be pardoned, that you should be accepted before God, that you should be saved from hell? Leave curious problems till salvation is secured.

July 12

If a man is thirsty, a rope and bucket are not in themselves of much use to him; but yet, if there is a well near at hand, the very thing that is wanted is a rope and a bucket, by means of which the water can be lifted. Faith is the bucket by means of which a man may draw water out of the wells of salvation, and drink to his heart's content. Use your faith now, and drink from the well of Bethlehem which Jesus filled for you.

July 13

The gardener takes his knife and prunes the fruit trees to make them bring forth more fruit. His little child comes trudging at his heels, and cries, "Father, I do not see that the fruit comes on the trees after you have cut them." No, dear child, it is not likely you would, for it is afterwards that the fruitfulness will come. In the season of fruit you shall see the golden apples which thank the knife for their birth. Graces which are meant to endure require time for their production; they are produced by chastening, but not at once.

July 14

Let my heart be tender, even if it must be softened by pain, for I would gladly know how to bind up my fellow's wound. Let mine eye have a tear ready for my brother's sorrows, even if in order to that I should have to shed ten thousand for mine own. Immunity from suffering would be a loss of power to sympathize, and that were to be deprecated beyond all things. Luther was right when he said affliction was the best book in the Christian's library.

July 15

Many are the ways which are not good. In the dry weather, as we crossed a road, a boy ran in front of us with his broom, pretending to sweep the path, but in reality raising a cloud of dust around us; and this reminds us of the men with new brooms of modern thought, who offer their services nowadays to clear the way for us, though all that they do is to create a blinding cloud of doubt and questioning. We prefer the plain man's pathway to heaven to the philosopher's downward road, however much he may sweep it.

July 16

In the Vatican we saw the renowned statue of the boy extracting a thorn from his foot. He was doing this when we first saw him; three years after he was attempting the same operation, and he will be found in like attitude fifty years hence. He is carved in marble, and therefore is excused for making no progress; but what shall be said of living individuals who year after year are trifling with imaginary difficulties, and never set foot on the road to heaven?

July 17

Lovers of antiquity, take care that your antiquity is antiquity. Let the old be old enough. With our own eyes we have seen "real antiques" in process of being made, and have observed the finishing touches as they gave the fine dark tinge to furniture of the middle ages fresh from the cabinet-maker's. The infallible Word of God is older than the supposed infallible Pope, the priesthood of the saints is older than the priestcraft of the clergy, the epistles are older than the thirty-nine articles, and the true church of God is older than any one of the sects.

July 18

"Our dying friends come o'er us like a cloud to damp our brainless ardours"; to make us feel that these poor fleeting toys are not worth living for; and that, as others pass away, so must we also be gone. Thus they help to cut us loose from this world, and urge us to take wing and mount towards the world to come. There are few sermons like deaths in our households; the departures of our beloved friends remind us of heaven, and show us the way.

July 19

A boat will only be needful when you reach a river. You shall have dying grace when dying time comes. The last enemy Will be destroyed, but not till the last. There is a great host of enemies to be fought today, and you may be content to let this one alone for a while. Of the times and seasons we are in ignorance, and therefore it is idle to speculate upon the time of our death: our wisdom is to be good soldiers of Jesus Christ as the duty of every day requires.

July 20

I read just now of a ship which was overtaken by a storm, and a mountainous wave went right over it, putting out the engine fires and sweeping away the wheel, so that the vessel lay like a log in the trough of the sea. Many a man has been water-logged by prosperity, a wave of wealth has swamped him, put out the fires of his zeal, taken away the steerage of his understanding, and left him helplessly to roll between the waves of worldliness and pride. "Lord, save us: we perish."

July 21

The few drops of bitterness in your cup today shall soon be rinsed out, and it shall be full of the nectar of heaven. Be content with your brown bread and hard fare a little while longer, for you will soon eat the delicacies of angels. Yea, and by faith you do even now feast upon the fat things full of marrow and the wines on the shelters well refined, which thy God sends to thee from the king's palace. Wherefore "let patience have her perfect work."

July 22

As the sun throws out its wealth of heat and light, casting it broadcast over all worlds,—even so does God flood the universe with the sunlight of his goodness, and his saints are made to bask in its beams. If you have ever been held back it is not by God. You have done it to yourself. Our receptive faculty may be small, but the Lord's giving disposition is infinite. Floods of mercy, oceans of love has he poured out for us.

July 23

When wealth grows with a man, his worldly estate is fatter; but if his soul becomes leaner he is a great loser. To gain silver and lose gold is a poor increase; but to gather for the body and lose for the soul is far worse. How earnestly might Israel have unprayed her prayers for flesh had she known what would come with the answer! The sighs of lust will have to be sighed over. We fret and fume till we have our desire, and then we fret still more because the attainment of it brings bitter disappointment.

July 24

That must be a terrible power which gathers strength from restraint, and feeds on that which should destroy it. Sin kills men by that which was ordained to life. It makes heaven's gifts the stepping-stones to hell, lights the way to perdition with the lamps of the temple, and makes the ark of the Lord, as in Uzzah's case, the messenger of death. Who would not flee to Christ, who alone can deliver from this fearful power?

July 25

Let your memory fly back to those early mornings with Christ when the dew was upon your soul, when the birds began to sing in your heart, and their notes had not yet grown stale to you. O the delicacies of the first days with Christ! O the sweetness of the love of our adoption! Do you not remember how you fed upon Christ to the very full, and rejoiced in him without ceasing? Look back and ask the Lord to renew your youth like the eagle's.

July 26

Thanksgiving does not belong alone to the eloquent, for he who can hardly put two words together can give thanks; nor is it confined to the rich, for the woman who had but two mites gave substantial thanks. The smoking flax may give thanks that it is not quenched, and the bruised reed may give thanks that it is not broken. Even the dumb may give thanks, their faces can smile a psalm; and the dying can give thanks, their placid brows beaming forth a hymn.

July 27

There must be life in us, or we cannot feed on the food around us; there must be an eye in the body, or light will be in vain; there must be grace within the soul, or else all the grace in means or ordinances cannot enrich us. When the ground is made good, the good seed yields a harvest; but often the barren soil devours all that the husbandman can put into it, and is none the better. "Ye must be born again."

July 28

It it would be marvelous to see a river leap up from the earth full-grown, what would it be to gaze upon a vast spring from which all the rivers of the earth should at once come bubbling up, a thousand of them born at a birth? What a vision it would be! Who can conceive it? And yet the love of God is that fountain from which all the rivers of mercy which have ever gladdened our race—all the rivers of grace in time, and of glory in eternity—take their rise.

July 29

If I neglect prayer for ever so short a time I lose all the spirituality to which I had attained; if I draw no fresh supplies from heaven the old corn in my granary is soon consumed by the famine which rages in my soul. When the caterpillars of indifference, the cankerworms of worldliness, and the palmerworms of self-indulgence lay my heart completely desolate, and make my soul to languish, all my former fruitfulness and growth in grace avail me nothing whatever. Therefore, O Lord, keep me every moment.

July 30

No bone in man's body knows how to rejoice till God has first broken it by a sense of sin. When it has been broken, and our gracious Physician of souls has set it with such skill that it gains more than its former strength, then the bone which had been broken rejoices exceedingly. Our healed wounds become mouths of praise unto the Most High, and every pang we have felt lives in the memory as an abiding argument for gratitude.

July 31

A naturalist when traveling in Brazil saw two white water-lilies growing side by side upon a lake; one of which was deliciously fragrant, while the other had the smell of coal tar. Alike fair to look upon, and growing in the same element, yet were they essentially different, and the scent betrayed them. How very like saints are certain professors! How constantly are they hearing the word! Yet there is a mysterious perfume of grace which they do not possess, and this deficiency reveals their real character.

August 1

Get your granary cleaned out, that the Lord may fill it with his good corn. Put the grist into the hopper and look for the wind to turn the sails of the mill. O you doubters, throw up the windows that the fresh breeze of the divine Spirit may blow in on your sickly faces. Expect that God is about to send the manna and have your omers ready. We shall see greater things than these if we awake to our duty and our privilege.

August 2

It were better to grow poorer than Lazarus, and more full of sores than he, than to become heartless and selfish. Rich, famous, learned, powerful, a man may be, but he is an object for the deepest pity if he has sacrificed the tenderness of his heart and become a sapless, leathery mortal, in whom every drop of the milk of human kindness is curdled. It is death above ground, it is the curse before the judgment, to be reduced to an unfeeling block of stone.

August 3

Have you ever had a painting which hung neglected in some back room? Did it one day strike you that you would have it framed and brought into a good light? When you saw it properly hung on the wall did you not exclaim, "I never saw the beauty of that picture before. How wonderfully it has come out?" Many a promise in God's word will never be noticed by you till it is set in a frame of new experience, and then you will be lost in admiration.

August 4

Yes, there are peculiar dangers in fine summer weather, from which we were free in winter. "It is the bright day that bringeth forth the snake." Fear and tremble you who abound with wealth, for yours is a post of peril, though you think not so. "The path is smooth that leadeth unto danger." Men in trouble ask our prayers, but those without trouble need them more. Let us pray.

August 5

Do not say, "I will get into communion with God when "I feel better," but long for communion now. It is one of the temptations of the devil to tell you not to read the promises when you are downcast; read them twice as much. When you feel least like praying, pray more, for you need it more; and when you feel very little like coming to God, cry out, "My God, I must be in a terrible state, or else I should have a greater longing after thee. Therefore I will not rest till I find thee out and come to thee.

August 6

Is not that a sweet verse of the 103rd Psalm,—"Who crowneth thee with loving-kindnesses and tender mercies"? The Lord makes kings of all his saints, and adorns them with better than golden coronets.

> "My crown is in my heart, not on my head;
> Not decked with diamonds and Indian stones,
> Nor to be seen; my crown is called content!
> A crown it is that seldom kings enjoy."

August 7

To perish in mid ocean seems not so hard a lot as to die with the white cliffs of Albion just before you: to die with the gospel ringing in our ears is still more sad. Never reckon the ship safe till it floats in the haven; never reckon a soul saved till it is actually "in Christ." The "almost persuaded" are often the last to be fully persuaded.

August 8

We read that Amalek fell upon Israel, and slew some of the hindmost of them. The experienced Christian will find much work for his weapons in aiding those poor doubting, desponding, wavering souls, who are in the rear as to faith, knowledge, and joy. These must not be left unaided, and therefore be it the business of well-taught saints to bear their standards among the hindmost. My soul, do thou tenderly watch to help the hindmost this day.

August 9

If we saw a poor wretch dying of cold we would divide our clothing with him. Shall we see sinners destitute of the robe of righteousness and not tell them of him who can clothe them in fair white linen? When a life is in peril, we use every exertion to effect a rescue; and yet this life is trivial compared with life eternal, and to be indifferent when men are perishing, is to act as if brotherly compassion had fled our bosoms.

August 10

"Harvest home" is not a joyous shout for the sluggard, who would not plow, and has nothing to reap. What can those hope for who have done nothing for God or their fellow men? The cottager harvests his little patch of corn with rejoicing, and believers with scanty opportunities shall receive their share of harvest joy; but woe to that man who professes godliness and yet is living for himself; he shall reap of the flesh corruption. What burning sheaves! What a harvest of shame! Will it be yours?

August 11

I seethe cemetery, or sleeping-place of the saints. They lie like soldiers sleeping around the captain's pavilion, where he spent the night, though he is up before them. The tomb of Jesus is the central grave of God's acre; it is empty now. but his saints lie buried all around their dear Redeemer's resting-place. Surely it robs the grave of its ancient terror when we think that Jesus slept in one of the chambers of the great dormitory of the sons of men.

August 12

If you want to catch flies, try honey; they will be more readily caught with that than with vinegar, at least if they are human flies. Put into your speech love rather than bitterness, and you will prevail. There are times when you must speak with all the sternness of an Elias; but, for all that, let the general current of your life, the natural overflow of your entire being, be thankfulness to God and kindness to men.

August 13

Who has not seen petrified sermons? Lifeless masses of orthodox doctrine: stones, and not bread! Who has not heard of petrified prayers? Blocks of granite in which warmth and life were the last things to be looked for. Have not gospel ordinances themselves in the hand of formalists become rather the gravestones of enthusiasm than firebrands to kindle its sacred flame? The world's greatest stumbling blocks are a lifeless church, a powerless ministry, and formal ordinances.

August 14

He who is the feeder of sparrows, will also furnish you with what you need. Sit not down in despair; hope on, hope ever. Take up the arms of faith against a sea of fears, "and by opposing end them." There is One above who cares for you, though all men deny you sympathy. He gave his Son to redeem you, and he will not suffer his redeemed to be famished. He will hear your cry. At any rate, try him and see.

August 15

You cannot logically institute comparisons where they do not hold. Rugged Peter has his place, and he is neither higher nor lower in value than polished Apollos. No one inquires which is the more useful—a needle or a pin, a wagon or a plow; they are designed for different ends, and they could not exchange places without serious detriment to their usefulness. Sit not in judgment upon others, lest thou judge their Maker.

August 16

It is not the scenery of this fair earth which is defiling, as ultra-spiritual simpletons would have us believe; neither is there anything in a lawful calling which necessarily interferes with holiness. From man proceeds the vileness; it comes neither from hill nor dale, nor streaming river, nor even from the din of machinery or the hum of crowds. Moral evil is the strange substance which poisons and pollutes, else earth might be the vestibule of heaven, and the labors of time a preparation for the engagements of eternity.

August 17

Truth was mighty before the best man living was born, and when he is carried to his grave with funeral music, sad and low, truth will not be buried with him. Fresh advocates will arise, and greater victories will be won. If you cut down that noble oak, there may spring up a dozen trees which else had been overshadowed. The removal of one man calls up others to the service; therefore, never despair because the faithful are removed.

August 18

Let all men beware of the tyranny of carnal passions, for no despots are so exacting as the appetites of the flesh. Suicide by one's own teeth is the meanest of deaths and involves a man in everlasting contempt; the cruelest of tyrants have not demanded this of their victims. By all that we value for time and for eternity, let us conquer fleshly appetites lest they conquer us. O Lord, be thou our helper.

August 19

A little lone plant in the forest had prepared a tiny flower, which as yet was not opened; yet the plant had no anxieties, but waited its time. Could it hope that the great sun would think of it and send its genial rays to bring its offspring to perfection? Yes, among the thick boughs the sunlight found its way, and the little flower unfolded itself, and shone like a monarch's crown. Even so will grace come to those who seek it, for the Lord forgets none who long for him.

August 20

Do the very weeds seek the beams of the sun and twist themselves about to face his brightness? Then am I rebuked, for I seek not thus my Lord. Without his light I cannot live, and shall I be content to die? Nay, my gracious Savior, help me to bask in thy love, and feel that heavenly sunshine which gladdens all the earth. I will look upward for your light, and when I receive it I will upward send the fragrance of my gratitude.

August 21

We saw in Venice a picture of St. Mark and other holy champions delivering the fair city from the devil, who had resolved to raise a great storm in the Adriatic, flood the lagoons and drown the inhabitants of the "Bride of the sea." The picture was all mere legend; but, for all that, the fable is capable of mirroring the grand truth that through the intercession of saints, and God's peculiar regard for them, cities and nations have often been saved.

August 22

As light shines from the center of the lantern through the glass, so when truth enlightens the heart its brightness soon beams forth in the outward life and conversation. You cannot improve the fruits of your orchard unless you make the trees better as to their secret juices, nor can a man's life be made Christlike unless his inner nature is divinely renewed.

August 23

Prayer is a telephone by which God speaks to man. His heaven is far away, but his voice sounds in our soul. Prayer is a phonograph: God speaks into our soul, and then our soul speaks out again what the Lord has spoken. If you do not pray, my brother, why then you have shut the gates of heaven against yourself, and there is neither coming in nor going out between you and your Lord; but prayer keeps up a heavenly commerce acceptable to God and enriching to your own soul.

August 24

All the blessings, all the mercies, all the comforts, all the riches which grace bestows flow to us from the well-head of eternal love through the covenant of which our Lord Jesus is the substance and the surety. No angels ascend or descend, save upon that ladder which Jacob saw which united man and his covenant God: that ladder our Lord Jesus pointed out to Nicodemus as being himself, the Son of man.

August 25

We must ever keep in mind that we are only channels for grace, we have no accumulated stores, but depend upon the continual flow of the divine stream. We must have an abiding union with the Fountain of all good, or we shall soon run dry; and become like the dry beds of mountain torrents filled with earth and stones. Blessed is the promise concerning the living water that it shall always flow; "in winter and summer shall it be."

August 26

If we would have wheat we must plow and sow; if we wish for flowers we must plant a garden, and tend it with care. Now, contentment is heaven's earthly paradise, and if we would enjoy its fruits and flowers we must cultivate it, and look well to the soil of our hearts. It is the new nature alone that can produce the flower called peace, and even then we must be especially careful lest ambition or unbelief should choke it.

August 27

We do not enjoy the high privilege of John to lean upon Jesus' bosom, nor of Paul to be caught up into the third heaven, but we have an equal share in the heart of our Redeemer if indeed we are believers in him. What we have not is by no means so great as what we have. The privileges coming to all the saints are infinitely greater than the small matters in which they differ.

August 28

Through the Spirit of God, the hope of heaven is a potent force for the production of virtue; it is the fountain of joyous effort, and the cornerstone of cheerful holiness. The man who has this hope in him goes about his work with vigor, for the joy of the Lord is his strength. He passionately fights against temptation, for his glorious hope, like a silver shield, repels the fiery darts of the adversary. He can labor without present reward, for he expects his recompense in the world to come.

August 29

Come, let us live while we live! Let us serve God to the utmost stretch of our manhood! Let us ask the Lord to brace our nerves, to string our sinews, and make us true crusaders, knights of the blood-red cross, consecrated men and women who, for the love we bear Christ's name, will count labor to be ease, and suffering to be joy, and reproach to be honor, and loss to be gain!

August 30

O unbelief, how strange a marvel thou art! We know not which most to wonder at, the faithfulness of God or the unbelief of his people. He keeps his promises a thousand times, and yet the next trial makes them doubt him. He is never a dry well, a passing meteor, or a melting vapor; and yet some professors are as continually vexed with anxieties, bothered by suspicions, and disturbed with fears, as if the promises of God were the mirage of the desert.

August 31

Conversion is a change of masters. Will we not do as much for our new master, the Lord Jesus, as we once did for our old tyrant lusts? We were very obedient and ardent servants unto sin, yielding our members to iniquity unto iniquity; shall we not now be equally earnest servants of righteousness unto holiness? Great Lord, be thou our helper, that as we once served evil with our whole nature, we may so serve thee, bowing our necks with delight to thine easy yoke.

September 1

Look at a pool of water when it stands still—it is mantled over with weed, stagnant and defiled! Give it vent, and let it run down yonder brook among the stones; leaping in little cascades on its way down to the river. It is alive now, and see how pure it grows, refining as it flows, because of its motion and life. So it must be with us: holy activity and progress are essential to purity.

September 2

Meditation is the tree of life in the midst of the garden of piety, and very refreshing is its fruit to the soul. As it is good towards man, so is it fair towards God. As the fat of the sacrifice was the Lord's portion, so are our best thoughts due to the Most High, and are most acceptable to him. We ought, therefore, to be much occupied with meditation, and the Lord himself should be our main subject. "My meditation of him shall be sweet."

September 3

When a swallow built its nest upon the tent of Charles V., the emperor generously commanded that the tent should not be taken down when the camp withdrew, but should remain until the young birds were ready to fly. Was there ever such gentleness in the heart of a soldier towards a poor bird which was not of his making, so shall the Lord deal with his creatures when in a child-like manner they put their trust in him!

September 4

Many passages of Scripture will never be made clear by the commentator; they must be expounded by experience. Many a text is written with secret ink, which must be held to the fire of adversity to make it readable. You see stars when looking up from the bottom of a well, though none may then be visible above ground, and in the deeps of trouble you will discern many a starry truth which would not else have been visible to you.

September 5

A little tampering with conscience is dangerous; it is like the dropping of a stitch, which may unravel all the work. We used to say in our childhood:—

"He who steals a single pin
Will live to steal a bigger thing."

The rhyme was bad, but the doctrine was true. If we violate conscience, even upon the smallest matter, we may come at last to have no conscience at all.

September 6

We are not far from being purged from our dross when we are perfectly willing to undergo any refining process which divine wisdom may appoint us. Self and sin have a great affinity, and till our selfishness is taken away our sin will not leave us; but when we can truly pray, "not as I will, but as thou wilt," then have we lost much of our alloy, and are ready to receive the image of the great King.

September 7

The wine pressed from the grapes of Sodom may sparkle and foam, but the dregs thereof are death; only that which comes from the clusters of the true vine may be safely received as the wine of the kingdom, which makes glad the heart of God and man. When Christ gives joy it is joy indeed; when the truth makes us glad it is true gladness. Holy joy is the joy of heaven, and that, be ye sure, is the very cream of joy.

September 8

As soldiers show their scars, and talk of battles, when they come at last to spend their old age in peace, so shall we in the dear land to which we are hastening speak of the faithfulness of God which brought us through all our conflicts. Therefore, as the contests of earth prepare food for heavenly conversation, we would not wish to be without them. We cannot wish to hear it said of the white-robed host, "These are they which came out of great tribulation," and then to feel that we did not share with them.

September 9

The petty sovereign of an insignificant tribe of aborigines every morning stalks out of his hovel, bids the sun good morrow, and points out to it with his finger the path he is to take for the day. Is this arrogance more contemptible than ours when we would dictate to God the course of his providence, and question the wisdom of his dealings with us?

September 10

When a man, in order to fulfill a promise, has to disarrange all his affairs, and, so to speak, to stop all his machinery, it proves that he is but a man, and that his wisdom and power are limited; but he is God indeed who, without reversing the engine of providence, or removing a single cog from the wheel of events, fulfills the desires of his people as they come up before him. The Lord is so omnipotent that he can work miracles without miracles, and change our state without changing his laws.

September 11

Preach up Christ, and down go the priests. The grand old Calvinistic truths, which are now kept in the background, are great cannons which will blow to pieces the heresies of the day, if they are plainly and persistently preached in harmony with the rest of revealed truth. Like ships of war in time of peace, the doctrines of grace have been laid up in ordinary; let us send them forth to pour red-hot shot into the enemy.

September 12

Wealth, or even moderate comfort, will often act like glue, and hold the birds of Paradise prisoners to carnal joys. When their nest is well lined men have little desire to depart and to be with Christ. It should not be so. If this world of vanity seems better to us than the realm of glory, our judgment is diseased, and the carnal nature is sadly hindering the aspirations of the divine life.

September 13

It is ours to abide where our great Captain has appointed our warfare till he himself shall release us from it. Like the dove which remained sitting upon her nest in the garden of Diomed when Pompeii was destroyed, if we are entrusted with the care of others we must sooner perish than forsake our charge. If Jesus has said, "Feed my lambs," we must not flee when the wolf cometh, but "Feed the flock of God which he hath purchased with his own blood."

September 14

When a man is privileged, by appointment, to be the purveyor of this or that to Her Majesty the Queen, he takes good care to let us know it. It is printed on his business cards and set up over his door. Connection with royalty is thought to dignify him. But, beloved, there is a King whom it is transcendent honor to serve—an honor which angels appreciate, which archangels delight in. That King is the once rejected Jesus of Nazareth.

September 15

Let the parlor and the drawing-room be adorned with cheerful piety; let the kitchen and the scullery be sanctified with unobtrusive godliness; let the shop and the office, the shed and the factory, be perfumed with unassuming holiness; let forge and bench and stall and lathe and spinning-jenny all be holiness unto the Lord, and the better times long sighed for will have come at last.

September 16

O you who are not eloquent, whose tongues will scarce respond to your thoughts, take heed that ye be not silent for the Lord, but bear your quiet witness for him. The smallest bell in the steeple is needed to complete the chime, and the tiniest bird would be missed from the choirs of the air if its note were hushed; therefore come thou forth, O least of all the brotherhood, for without thine aid the work of the Father's household will not be fully done.

September 17

There is a close kinship in trouble. When Christians are in affliction it is delightful to observe how they that fear the Lord speak often one to another. A poor old woman who knows the things of God by experience becomes of more value to you in your hour of grief than the dainty gentleman whose company bewitched you in the past. Let all who are mourning open their hearts to true brethren, and in sympathy they will find solace.

September 18

The burnt child dreads the fire, but the burnt sinner lovingly returns to his sin. Gray hairs ought to be a crown of glory, but too often they are fools' caps. When young sinners waste the prime of life and miss the early joy of religion they are fools. But what is he who hath one foot hanging over the mouth of hell, and yet continues without God and without Christ, a trifler on the brink of eternity?

September 19

When a surgeon, wearing the red cross, goes to the battlefield after a conflict he is guided to his compassionate work by the groans of the wounded. When he hears a cry he does not inquire, "Was that a Russian or a Turk, and what does he mean?" A cry is good Russian, and excellent Turkish, too; it is part of the universal tongue. Whatever language, O sinner, you use, uncouth or refined, if it rises from your heart, the great Physician understands you without need of an interpreter.

September 20

A cheerful believer once remarked that the Christian life may be described as "good, better, best,"— "the shining light, that shineth more and more unto the perfect day but close researches into our own heart lead us to apply very different adjectives to our carnal nature, for this, to our apprehension, is "bad, worse, worst." All is light in the Lord, but all is darkness in self; in the Lord Jehovah have we righteousness and strength; in ourselves nothing but sin and weakness.

September 21

The carpenter's gimlet makes but a small hole, but it enables him to drive a great nail. May we not here see a representation of those minor departures from the truth which prepare the minds of men for grievous errors, and of those thoughts of sin which open a way for the worst of crimes! Beware, then, of Satan's gimlet.

September 22

The sweetest songs are those which celebrate deliverance from the pit of corruption. Did you ever keep a finch in a cage, and then think to yourself that it was hard to rob it of its liberty? Did you open the cage door and let it fly? Oh, but if you could have heard it sing when it had fairly escaped, you would have heard the best finch-music in all the wood. When a poor soul is set free by God from the dungeon of despair, what songs it pours forth!

September 23

A gardener does not go through the forest and prune the wildflowers, the blackberries, and the hawthorns; he does not care enough about them. But see how he purges the vines and prunes the fruit trees! My gardener cut my roses back so very much that I thought there would be no flowers; but when I saw the luxuriant roses I understood that he and his knife knew more than I. Good roses must suffer the knife, and God's saints must be afflicted.

September 24

After the showers have fallen from the dark and lowering skies, how pleasant is the breath of nature, how delightfully the sun peers through the thick trees, transforming all the raindrops to sparkling gems; and even so, after a shower of troubles, it is marvelously delightful to feel the divine refreshings of the Lord, speedily transforming every tear into a jewel of delight, and satisfying the soul with soothing peace.

September 25

If you grow till you are less than nothing, you are full grown; but few have reached that stage. If you grow till Christ is everything to you, you are in your prime; but, alas, how far short of this do most men fall! The Lord bring you to that highest of all growths—to be daily coming to Christ; always empty in yourself, but full in him; always weak in yourself, but strong in him; always nothing in self, but Christ your perpetual all in all.

September 26

The life of each one of the redeemed contains a world of wonders, and therefore each should render a wealth of praises. Who can recount the marvels of grace which the Lord has wrought for his church? They are as high above our thoughts as the heavens are high above the earth. When shall these silent tongues learn to praise him? Our harps are cobwebbed with inexcusable neglect. "Awake, my glory; awake, psaltery and harp: I myself will awake early."

September 27

A forgiven sinner decked out in the flaunting garments of a worldling casts suspicion upon her own pardon; if she had ever been renewed in heart, would she, could she, adorn herself after the manner of a Jezebel? It is hard to think of a disciple of the Lord wasting her substance upon personal decoration. Can you imagine a Mary or a Dorcas bedizened like a foolish woman?

September 28

There is a trying word and a delivering word, and we must bear the one till the other comes to us. How meekly Joseph endured his afflictions, and with what fortitude he looked forward to the clearing of his slandered character! It will be well if, under similar trials, we are able to imitate him and come forth from the furnace as thoroughly purified as he was, and as well prepared to bear the yet sterner ordeal of honor and power.

September 29

Plants when they are pot-bound become poor weak things, and so do men's hearts when they are earth-bound by their riches. As a traveler finds it hard to move when his feet stick in the mud of a miry way, so do men make small progress heavenward when they are hindered by their wealth. Happy is that man who has riches but does not allow riches to have him: who uses wealth, and does not idolize it, but seasons all with the Word of God and prayer.

September 30

How delicious to feel your soul on the wing and full of life, like the birds in spring, which are always singing and flitting from bough to bough, full of energy and pleasure. To be constant, instant, eager in prayer and praise—this is health, vigor, and delight. It is not always so; but when we are in such a state our days are "as the days of heaven upon earth."

October 1

The more saintly a saint becomes, the more will he mourn over the sin which dwells in his members, and this will set him longing and thirsting after more grace. When our old unbelief begins to wither our faith, when our natural indifference commences to dry up our life, when our doubts parch the pastures of our hope, and our sins drain the wells of our consolation, it is little wonder if we come into a dry and thirsty land, where no water is.

October 2

You and I may travel in lines almost parallel, and we may therefore know each other's griefs, and tenderly sympathize; but there is a turning in my life which you have never reached. No one man is the exact replica of another, and yet our Lord Jesus is in full sympathy with each one of us. What a wonderful manhood is his! It rises far above us, and yet is at the side of each one of us in a marked and special manner.

October 3

Just as the birds, when the eggs are in the nest, have upon them a natural feeling that they must sit on those eggs, and that they must feed those little fledglings which will come from them; so if God calls you to win souls, you will have a natural love for them, a longing wrought in you by the Holy Spirit, so that the whole force of your being will run out in that direction, seeking the salvation of men.

October 4

Two soldiers wear the same regimentals, and they talk equally loudly of what they will do when the enemy shall come; but the battle tests and proves them, and then each man is made known. Some peculiar phase of the conflict sets them in divergent positions, but till the battle comes how easy it is for the coward to play the hero, while the hero holds his tongue. Boasting is the language of fools. It is written, "Let this mind be in you which was also in Christ Jesus," and he was meek and lowly in heart.

October 5

There is always variety in scenery; diversities of form and color are seen in every land. You never saw two hills molded to the same pattern, or two rivers that wound after the same fashion from their source down to the sea: nature abhors monotony. So is the work of the Holy Spirit manifold and various. In the work of conversion there is a sameness of purpose, but no uniformity of ways and means.

October 6

O ambitious man, you that run after something, and you cannot tell what it is that can gratify your immortal spirit, turn to the cross, for at the foot of it there springs a sacred fount of soul-satisfying delight, and if you will but stoop and drink, your ambition shall quench its thirst, for you will find honor, and glory, and immortality in Christ. Jesus says, "he that drinks of the water that I shall give him shall never thirst."

October 7

When Saul went forth to seek his father's donkeys and brought them not home, but met with Samuel and so found a kingdom, did he set up a lamentation? Would he have been pleased if others had sympathized with his sad lot? Even so when we miss our worldly objects, and by the trial are led to find the kingdom of God, shall we be sorry or ask others to grieve our misfortune? Nay, rather we sing over the thrice blessed troubles which lead us to eternal riches.

October 8

To make gold out of dross would be a miracle, and it is the glory of God to work miracles by turning his enemies into friends. In this we should strive to be like him. To change an angry foe into a fervent friend is a worthy imitation of him who makes the lion to lie down with the lamb. Love is the great transformer, the real wonder-worker; it will tame the wildest, and baffle the malicious. Have you tried in vain to overcome your enemy? Try love, and mark the result of the trial.

October 9

A great preacher was wont to say, "Hang upon him that did hang upon the cross." In truth, this is the essence of saving faith; and he who has it is saved, for he is joined unto the Savior, and till the Savior falls he falls not. But mind you hang there wholly, for one hand on the Lord Jesus and another on yourself will bring you a double ruin, for mocking him and idolizing your own fancied merits.

October 10

As long as there is a particle of selfishness remaining in us, it will mar our sweet enjoyment of Christ; and until we get a complete riddance of it our joy will never be unmixed with grief. We must dig at the roots of our selfishness to find the worm which eats our happiness. The soul of the believer will always pant for this serene condition of passive surrender, and will not content itself until it has thoroughly lost itself in the sea of divine love.

October 11

If you put upon a horse a golden saddle and a silken bridle he is not one whit the fitter for a journey; and if you lay upon him a pack of silver ingots he will even travel all the worse. Rank cannot make a man the better Christian, nor is wealth an assistance towards holiness. Why then do men seek honor and fortune as if these were the chief good? If they were wise they would covet earnestly the best gifts.

October 12

Mnemosyne, the goddess of memory, is also the mother of the muses. It is from the memory of the Lord's great goodness that we learn to sing his praises. Remember then the loving-kindness of the Lord and forget not all his benefits. Does not divine love in every one of its favors present us with a forget-me-not, and say, "Receive this in remembrance of me."

October 13

The experienced believer is in advance of younger brethren if his experience has developed itself in a deeper, steadier, and more abiding love of Christ. He is to the babe in grace what the oak is to the sapling—more firmly rooted, more strong in heart, and broader in spread; his love, too, is to the affection of the new convert what the deep-rolling river is to the sparkling brook. Especially is this the case if like a veteran he has been in the wars and borne the brunt of battle.

October 14

Maturity in grace makes us willing to part with the world. The green apple needs a sharp twist before it will relinquish its hold upon the bough, but the ripe fruit parts readily from the wood. So, too, maturity in grace makes it easier to part with life itself; the unripe pear is scarcely beaten down with much labor, while its mellow companion drops readily into the hand with the slightest shake. Men who are ripe for glory quit this mortal life without regret, yea, even with readiness.

October 15

The tracks of ancient rivers have been found all dry and desolate; but the streams which take their rise on the mountains of divine sovereignty and infinite love shall never fail. Generations melt away; but the course of grace is unaltered. That stream may well say—

"Men may come and men may go,
But I go on forever."

October 16

We were told of a fresh road, and we tried it, and found it foul at its entrance, miry in its progress, and abrupt in its termination, landing us nowhere. The old road is steep, and tires our knees, but we shall keep to it, in future, for it leads to the town. The doctrines of grace and puritanic practice are not attractive to the flesh, but they are safe, they have been long tried, and their end is peace. Others may say, "We will not walk therein," but as we have found rest for our souls in the good road, we shall keep to it.

October 17

While craving for something unusual we may be neglecting that which infinite wisdom has put within our reach, like the foolish child which cries for the moon, and forgets to eat its apple. There are many who in their sincerely earnest desires to gain some "token for good" forget that earnestness of the Spirit which dwells in their own bosoms, and thus they miss present comforts, and are weakened for present duties. They sit in chains forged by their own fancy, when they might walk at large.

October 18

There are lines of weakness in the creature which even grace does not efface. "When the peacock is proud of his fine feathers," says old Master Dyer, "he may be humbled by seeing his black feet." And so, whenever the brightest Christian begins to be proud of his graces, there will be sure to be something about him which will remind others as well as himself that he is yet in the body.

October 19

On the summit of Snowdon stands a wooden platform. Now, I can well imagine that under a little extra weight this frail frame shakes, and nervous persons imagine that the mountain moves. So do some believers stand aloft on their poor attainments, and when these fail, then they dream that the ground of their faith is removed. "Nevertheless, the foundation of God standeth sure." Better far to keep on the solid rock of ages and forego all attempts to rise beyond a simple dependence upon free and sovereign grace.

October 20

My soul, I charge thee, lay up you treasure in the only secure cabinet; store your jewels where you can never lose them. Put your all in Christ; set all your affections on his person, all your hope in his merit, all your trust in his efficacious blood, all your joy in his presence; and then you may laugh at loss, and defy destruction. Remember that all the flowers in the world's garden fade by turns, and the day comes when nothing will be left but the black, cold earth.

October 21

In some parts of the world there are not long twilights before the break of day, but the sun leaps up in a moment, darkness flies, and light reigns: so is it with many of the Lord's redeemed: as in a moment their ashes are exchanged for beauty. Faith is the great transformer. Will you cast yourself now, whether you live or die, upon the precious blood and merits of the Savior Jesus Christ? If you will do so you are saved; your sins, which are many, are at once forgiven you.

October 22

Though godliness has the promise of the life that now is, yet this is not our rest, and woe unto us if we try to make it so. All the trees in this forest are marked for the axe. Build your nests, my brethren, on the everlasting rocks, where God's eagles have their nests, high above the reach of time and change, in the eternal purpose and everlasting love of God; for your portion is not in the present, neither may you seek it there.

October 23

A religious profession requires grace to sustain it. A company which begins business without cash will soon lose even its nominal capital. It will, in fact, lose what it never had; thus thoroughly illustrating the words of our Lord, "he that hath not, from him shall be taken away that which he hath"; and, as in a parable, setting before us the result of pretending to be Christians if we have no grace to maintain our profession.

October 24

The sky was darkened, storm-clouds gathered like hosts for the battle, the dread artillery of heaven shook the everlasting hills. We hastened home, dreading the tempest. But it came not upon our sheltered abode; it spent itself among the mountains. Thus has the righteous wrath of God poured out itself upon the Lord Jesus, who like a glorious mountain-summit has borne the brunt of the storm, that we upon whom it would otherwise have burst might dwell in perfect peace.   :

October 25

You, brother, may be as a bundle of the best corn. Be grateful, but remember that you will feel the "sharp thrashing instrument having teeth." And you, my brother, may be one of the tender seeds of the Master's garden. Be grateful, for you shall feel a lighter flail than others; but do not boast therein, for you may almost regret that gentler flail, which proves that you are of lighter stuff, though still true grain of the Master's sowing.

October 26

Fire will not remain in a single coal, but if many be laid together it will be long before the fire is clean gone. The communion of saints is their mutual conservation. A single tree may not afford much shelter for a traveler, but he will rest beneath the thick boughs of the grove; so will Jesus often remain longest where many of "the trees of the Lord" are planted. The fellowship of Christians preserves their fellowship with Christ. Go to the assemblies of the saints, if you would keep the arm of the King of saints.

October 27

When a pump is dry you must pour water down it first, and then you will get water; and so, Christian, when you are dry, go to God; ask him to give you grace, and then you will manifest grace; beg him to shed abroad his joy in your heart, and then your joy will be full.

October 28

If believers were lost, God would lose more than they, for the glory of his name would be tarnished. If I am a sheep and I am lost, I am a great loser certainly; but then I am not my own, but belong to the great Shepherd, and he has lost me, and so is a loser, too. If I am a member of Christ's body, and am lost, my Head is a loser, too; for then his body is incomplete. The church is "the fullness of him that fills all in all"; and the Lord Jesus were not a perfect Christ if he lost the lowliest member of his body.

October 29

Evidences of grace without Christ are like unlit candles, which afford no light: like fig-trees with leaves only, devoid of fruit; like purses without gold, and like barns without wheat: they have great capabilities of comfort, but without Jesus they are emptiness itself. Evidences are like conduit-pipes—they are sometimes the channels of living water, but if the supply from the fountain head be cut off from them, their waters utterly fail.

October 30

"There's something in me that reproves my fault." Thank God it is so, for conscience is the drag upon the wheel to stay the chariot in its mad career. Listen to the inward warning. He was a fool who shot his watchdog for disturbing his sleep, and so left himself a prey to the burglar; treat not your conscience so, but be grateful for its admonitions and cheerfully obey them.

October 31

It is pleasant when sunning oneself amid the orange groves to see the mountains crowned with snow, for it reminds you of the cold which you are escaping. It will add a zest to the believer's joy if he remembers the wretched estate of sin from which he is delivered, and the yet more terrible condition of eternal condemnation to which he was once hastening. Bask in the beams of love, and bless the Lord that, though you were sometime darkness, you are now light in the Lord.

November 1

It is of no use to hope that we shall be well rooted if no rough winds pass over us. Those gnarlings on the root of the oak, and those strange twistings of the branches, all tell of the many storms which have swept over it, and they are also indicators of the depth into which the roots have forced their way. So through divine grace the Christian is made strong and firmly rooted by all the trials and storms of life.

November 2

He who boasts of grace has little grace to boast of. Some who do this imagine that their graces can sustain themselves, forgetting that the stream must flow constantly from the fountain head, or else the brook will soon be dry. If a continuous supply of oil comes not to the lamp, though it burn brightly today it will smoke tomorrow, and noxious will be its scent. Take heed that you glory not in your graces, but let all your glorying and confidence be in Christ and his strength, for only so can you be kept from falling.

November 3

While a man can pray he is never far from light; he is at the window, though, perhaps, as yet the curtains are not drawn aside. The man who can pray has the clue in his hand by which to escape from the labyrinth of affliction. Like the trees in winter, we may say of the praying man, when his heart is greatly troubled, "his substance is in him when he has cast his leaves." Isaiah 6:13. Therefore, troubled one, "pray without ceasing."

November 4

We toiled up a cold ascent, shivering in the shade, and we were cheered in doing so, for on the summit stood a cross gleaming in the sun. No sooner had we reached that cross than we were in the full warmth of an Italian day. Courage, poor sinner; press forward to the cross of Jesus; sunlight is there, and all the genial summer of God's love shall smile around you. Believe and live.

November 5

Love is the marrow of the bones of fidelity, the blood in the veins of piety, the sinew of spiritual strength— yea, the life of sincere devotion. He that has love can no more be motionless than the aspen in the gale, the dry leaf in the hurricane, or the spray in the tempest. As well may hearts cease to beat as love cease to labor. Love is instinct with activity, it cannot be idle; it is full of energy, it cannot content itself with littles: it is the well-spring of heroism, and great deeds are the gushings of its fountain.

November 6

Southwell says concerning Mary, "That she chose the best part is beyond all question, good Lord, since she made choice of nothing else but thee." It was good to be willing to sit at a wise man's feet to learn; it was better still to choose Jesus for her teacher, and it was best of all to abide in the learner's place, altogether taken up with attending to his gracious words.

November 7

There are odd people to be met with who will go to heaven, we have no doubt; for they are pilgrims on the right way, but we have no wish for much of their company on the road. They are crossed-grained and crabbed, with a something about them that one's nature can no more delight in than the palate can take pleasure in nauseous medicine. They are a sort of spiritual hedgehogs; they are alive and useful, and no doubt they illustrate the wisdom and patience of God, but they are wretched company.

November 8

When rain falls in its needed season, we scarcely stay to return thanks for the boon; but if it be withheld, how do we bless the drops and thank the God of heaven for them. Sunlight is never more grateful than after a long watch in the midnight blackness; Christ's presence is never more acceptable than after a time of weeping his absence. It is a sad thing that we should need to lose our mercies to teach us to be grateful for them.

November 9

Dear friend, whether you die as soon as you are born again, or remain on earth for many years, is comparatively a small matter, and will not materially alter your indebtedness to divine grace. In the one case the great Husbandman will show how he can bring his flowers speedily to perfection; and in the other he will prove how he can preserve them in blooming beauty, despite the frosts and snows of earth's cruel winter: in either case your experience will reveal the same love and power.

November 10

It is poor evidence of a renewed heart when a man must always be the lead horse in the team. He who knows the Lord loves to sit at Christ's feet: the lower the place the better for him. He is glad even to wash the saints' feet, yea, he thinks it an honor to keep the door. If you Christian people must dispute about precedence, always fight for the lowest place. If you aspire to be last and least you will have few competitors; there will be no demand for a poll; for the lowest seat is undisputed.

November 11

Though some days may add but little to the heap, yet little by little it increases to a mountain. Little experiences, if well husbanded, will soon make us rich in love. Though the banks of the river shelve but gently, yet he that is up to the ankles shall find the water covering his knees, if he do but continue his wading. Blessed is the saint whose love to his Lord has become confirmed with his years, so that his heart is fixed, and fired, and flaming.

November 12

Neglect of family prayer will work great evil in our households. The practice of family prayer is the castle of Protestantism. It is the grand defense against all attacks by a priestly caste, who set up their temples and tell us to pray there, and pray by their mediation. Nay, but our own houses are temples, and every man is a priest at home. This is a brazen wall of defense against superstition and priestcraft. Family prayer is the nutriment of family piety, woe to those who allow it to cease.

November 13

If I were at any time to be subject to a surgeon's knife I should feel sure that if he wounded me he would see me through the operation, and do his utmost for my restoration. Now, God is the great Surgeon of men's souls, and sometimes he cuts to the very bone; but he never means to kill. He never takes the knife of discipline, except with the intent to bind up every wound he makes, and set the man upon his feet again, "saved in the Lord with an everlasting salvation."

November 14

Men put dark colors into the picture to make the lights more apparent; and God uses our black griefs to heighten the brightness of his mercies. The weeping of penitence is the sowing of a harvest of joy. Spiritual sorrow is the architect of the temple of praise; or, at least, like Hiram, it floats on its seas the cedars for the pillars of the beautiful house. To appreciate mercies we must feel miseries.

November 15

Nobody, I suppose, teaches the young mother how to manage her first child, and yet somehow or other it is done, because she loves it. It is wonderful to me how a widow with a swarm of children provides for them all. I cannot tell how, but the love she bears them leads her to make exertions which would seem impossible to anyone else, and the little ones are by some means housed and fed and clothed. If you have love enough, you can win any man to Jesus by God's grace.

November 16

I know what it is to suffer from terrible depression of spirit; yet at the very moment when it has seemed to me that life was not worth anything I have been perfectly peaceful with regard to all the greater things. The surface of the mind may be lashed into storm and yet down deep in the caverns of one's inmost consciousness all is still. There are earthquakes upon this globe, and yet our planet pursues the even tenor of its way, and the like is true in the little world of a believer's nature.

November 17

The emancipated galley-slave may forget the day which heard his broken chains rattle on the ground; the pardoned traitor may fail to remember the moment when the axe of the headsmen was averted by a pardon; and the long despairing mariner may not recollect the moment when a friendly hand snatched him from the hungry deep: but O hour of forgiven sin! Moment of perfect pardon! Our soul shall never forget you while her life and being shall remain.

November 18

Let others do what they will, but God forbid that I should glory save in the cross of our Lord Jesus Christ. I see certain of my brethren fiddling away at the branches of the tree of vice with their wooden saws; but, as for the gospel, it lays the axe at the root of every tree in the whole forest of evil, and if it be fairly received into the heart it cuts up the briars at once, and causes instead of them the fir tree, the pine tree, and the box tree together to spring up and flourish, to beautify the house of our Master's glory.

November 19

It is usually true that second thoughts are best, but it is not so in the service of our Lord. The first suggestions of love, like the first beams of the morning, are not to be excelled for beauty and freshness. Good deeds had better be done at once, without a second thought. "I consulted not with flesh and blood," said the apostle; Is it a right thing? Is it for Jesus? Then delay not.

November 20

Men know not the gold which lies in the mine of Christ Jesus, or surely they would dig in it night and day. The person of Christ strikes eloquence dumb when it would describe him, and it palsies the artist's arm when with fair colors he would portray him. It would baffle the greatest sculptor to produce the image of the altogether lovely One, even were it possible to chisel it in a massive block of diamond.

November 21

Though God has made this round world exceeding fair, yet no work of creation reflects so much of his highest glory as the manifestation of his grace in a pardoned sinner. If you arrange all the stars around, and if it be so that every star is filled with a race of intelligent beings, yet, methinks, among unfallen existences you will discover no such marvel as a forgiven sinner.

November 22

Lost on a dreary moor, the wanderer discovers his cottage by the light in the window casting a gleam over the darkness of the waste; so also must we find out "our dwelling-place" by the lamps of promise which our Savior hath placed in the windows of his word. The handkerchiefs brought from the person of Paul healed the sick; surely the promises, which are the garments of Christ, will avail for all diseases.

November 23

If you were going home today, and saw a number of boys throwing stones and breaking windows, you might not interfere with them; but if you saw your own lad among them I will be bound you would fetch him out, and make him repent of it. If God sees sinners going on in their evil ways, he may not punish them now, for he will deal out justice to them in another state; but if he sees one of his own elect sinning, he will soon make him rue the day.

November 24

There is no power in this world so vital, so potent at this day as the power of Christ. I say nothing just now of heavenly or spiritual things; but I speak only of temporal and moral influences; even in these the cross is to the front. He of whom Voltaire said that he lived in the twilight of his day, is going from strength to strength. The infidel truly said that it was the twilight, but it was the twilight of the morning, and the full noon is coming.

November 25

What slow-coaches we have to deal with. You travel by broad-wheeled wagon to heaven, even you who rush along by express-train in the world's business. Yes, you must attend to the world, and my Lord and Master may wait your convenience, as temporizing Felix long ago desired; but this should not be. As soon as you know what your Lord would have you to do, every moment of unnecessary delay is a sin.

November 26

Who can place his own character side by side with the two tablets of the divine law without perceiving that he has fallen far short of the standard? When the law enters the soul, it is like light in a dark room revealing the dust and the dirt, unseen before. It is the test which detects the presence of the poison of sin in the soul. "I was alive without the law once," said the apostle, "but when the commandment came, sin revived, and I died." Our comeliness utterly fades away when the law blows upon it.

November 27

A retiring disposition is a small virtue in a soldier of Christ. The soldier who retired in the day of battle was shot for a coward. Never be retiring when duty or danger summon you to the front. It is ill to have the face of a lion and the heart of a deer. Disreputable things are sometimes disguised in words polite; so diffidence may be dastardly, and caution may be cowardly. Be very valiant for the Lord of hosts.

November 28

As to the revelation with which our heavenly Father has so graciously favored us, how little have we gazed upon it in the clear daylight of its own glory! Our prejudices, fancies, follies, iniquities, unbeliefs, and vanities have raised a November mist through which heaven's own stars can scarcely dart their cheering rays. There is light enough abroad if the dense fog would suffer it to reach us; but for want of the wind of heaven to chaste away the obscuring vapors, we walk in twilight, and see but glimmerings of truth.

November 29

While sick men take two kinds of medicine, there is little hope of a cure, especially if the two draughts are compounded of opposing ingredients; the bird which lives on two trees builds its nest on neither; and the soul halting between grace and works can never find rest for the sole of its foot. Perhaps, my reader, a secret and well-nigh imperceptible self-trust is the very thing which shuts out Christ from thy soul.

November 30

Our London fog finds its way through your clothing, your flesh, and your bones, into your very marrow; and the sinner's uneasiness is very like it. He tries to keep out the feeling of despondency and apprehension, by a thousand inventions which the world calls pleasure; but he cannot do it. He is "without God," and he is consequently without rest. He is well mirrored by those shivering, half-clad, hungry creatures whom we see in a foggy night hurrying on to get a cold seat on the workhouse doorstep.

December 1

Despair is unreasonable. Learn a lesson from the naked boughs, barren as lances, among which the wind is sighing. These shall yet again robe themselves in graceful foliage and boast new charms and ampler spread. Why not the like with you, if you will but look up and hope in God, whose love will shed a spring-tide over your soul, yea, bring you to a summer of supreme delight.

December 2

The bitter breath of winter is the creator of many beauties. See how the dead leaves are frosted with silver or filigreed as with the same precious metal. Broken twigs and rotten branches are transformed into silver rods and bars under frost's magic fingers. When the winter of affliction is upon us our commonest mercies become invaluable, and forgotten words of comfort grow precious to our souls. Thus even sorrow has its charms.

December 3

The best religion in the world is that which smiles at the table, works at the sewing-machine, and is pleasant in the chimney corner, and amiable in the drawing-room. Give me the religion which blacks boots and shines them well; cooks the food so that it may be eaten; measures out yards of calico, and does not make them half-an-inch short; sells a hundred yards of an article, and does not label ninety as a hundred, as many tradespeople do. That is true Christianity which affects the whole of our behavior.

December 4

The astronomer believes that the most erratic comet will yet accomplish its journey, and revisit our sphere; but Christian people often give up backsliders for lost when they have not wandered one-half the distance from the center of light and life. We find an excuse for inaction in the fancied hopelessness of sinners; while our fastidious delicacy pleads the fear of pollution, seeking to mask at once our indolence and pride. If we had right views of ourselves, we should judge none too base to be reclaimed.

December 5

Where is the squirrel now, who but a little while ago all full of play was leaping from bough to bough? God hath laid him asleep in the hollow of a tree, "on a bed of wool or matted leaves." He is safe enough, and snugly hidden from the howling blast. And will not God care for you should the worst come to the worst? Yea, he will hide you in a refuge of his own preparing. Only trust in him and dread no ill.

December 6

He that is down so low as to be wholly submissive, will find that divine justice will not smite him. Mercy always flies near the ground. The flower of grace grows in the valley of humility. The star of hope shines in the night of our self-despair. The hand of justice spares the sinner who has thrown away both the sword of his rebellion and the plumes of his pride. If we will do and be anything or everything, so that we may win Christ, we shall soon find him to be everything to us.

December 7

No ship was ever wrecked by the captain's over-anxiety in taking his longitude and latitude; but the wailing wind bears sad witness to the fate of careless mariners who forgot their chart, and wantonly steered onward to rocks which prudent foresight would easily have avoided. Let us not sleep as do others, but rouse ourselves to persevering watchfulness by the solemn consideration that if we be at last mistaken in our soul's condition, the error can never be amended.

December 8

Who envies the Russian Empress that palace of ice which she once so proudly piled? Was it not a fit image of the glory of this world? "It smiled, but it was cold;" it was bright but transient, clear as crystal but utterly devoid of comfort. Give me a humble lot and the fair sun of holy joy to warm its narrow chamber. He whom God loves dwells in a palace brighter far, which never melts away.

December 9

Let not boyish anxieties and juvenile repentances be lightly regarded. He incurs a fearful amount of guilt who promotes the aim of the Evil One by trampling upon a tender conscience in a child. No one knows the age of the youngest responsible child, and therefore none can tell at what age children are capable of conversion. We can bear our personal testimony to the fact that grace operates on some minds in the very dawn of reason.

December 10

As on the frail raft the almost skeleton mariners, having long ago devoured their last morsel, raise themselves with all their remaining strength to catch a glimpse of a passing sail, if haply it may bring relief, so does the awakened sinner receive with eagerness the message of coming grace. He might have scorned the terms of mercy once; but, like a city starved into a surrender, he is now too glad to receive peace at any price. Is it so with you? Then grace is near at hand.

December 11

All earth-born consolations are in their essence fleeting and in their existence short-lived; they are as brilliant and as evanescent as the rainbow hues of a soap-bubble; but as for the consolations which God gives to his people, they fade not, neither do they lose their freshness. They can stand all tests—the shock of trial, the flame of persecution, the lapse of years; nay, they can even endure death itself.

December 12

None are nearer mercy's door than those who are farthest from their own; none are more likely to get a good word from Jesus than they who have not one word to say for themselves. He that is clean escaped from the hands of self has not a step between himself and acceptance. It is a good sign of a high tide of grace when the sands of our own righteousness are covered. Take heart that Christ loves you when you have no heart for the work of self-saving.

December 13

All ships do not make speedy voyages; the peculiar build of the vessel, the winds, the waves, and the mistakes of the captain all affect the time of the journey. The Lord can, when it is his good pleasure, bring convicted sinners at once into the haven of peace; but at times he delays relief for purposes which, though we know not now, we shall know hereafter. "Be not afraid; only believe."

December 14

The essence of gardening lies in thinking in time. In the depth of winter, the gardener has an eye to spring and summer, and indeed many plants require him to look two years ahead. Why is it that men will never look forward? They know that there is a future state, and yet they think no more of it than the steer fattening for Christmas. Reader, since God has given you the intelligence of a man, use it, and do not live like the ox of the stall.

December 15

A dark cloud is no sign that the sun has lost his light; and black convictions are no arguments that God has laid aside his mercy. Destruction and wrath may thunder, but mercy can out-speak them. Get beneath the tree whereon Jesus died, and not a drop of the shower of wrath will fall on you. Fear not to go, for the cherubim which you see are not guards to prevent your approach, but ministers to welcome your coming.

December 16

Trees are not always green, the sap sleeps in the winter. Our souls have their winters too; their life is not all summer. We should always grow, but we cannot flower every day; and if we bear fruit, yet is not the fruit always ripe, nor does the ripeness perpetually wear the same delicate bloom. Till we are perfected we shall not stay at our highest point, else were earth turned to heaven, and the variableness of time merged in the immutability of eternity.

December 17

Life is so brief that no man can afford to lose an hour of it. It has been well said that if a king should bring us a great heap of gold, and bid us take as much as we could count in a day, we should make a long day of it; we should begin early in the morning, and in the evening we should not withhold our hand. Now, to win souls, or to grow in grace, or to commune with God, is far nobler work; how is it that we so soon withdraw from it?

December 18

Prayer is one of the royal musicians; and although many do prefer his brother, who is called praise, yet this one has always had an equal share of the king's favor. His lute plays so sweetly that once upon a time the heavens smiled with sunshine for the space of three years and six months at the sound of it; and when the melodious tune was changed, the same skies wept for joy, till abundance of rain descended on the earth.

December 19

The heavenly-minded man is not content to pluck the wild flowers of false philosophy, nor is he eager to reach the tempting blossoms of speculation blooming on the edge of the cliffs which skirt the sea of the unrevealed; but he anxiously looks around for the rose of Sharon, the lily of the valley. He who seeks first and foremost after this choicest of all flowers, and would know Jesus beyond all things else, shall have all other wisdom added unto him.

December 20

Small inconsistencies are dangerous. Little thorns make great blisters, little moths destroy fine garments, and little frivolities and minor faults rob religion of a thousand joys. O professor, too little separated from sinners, you know not what you lose by your conformity to the world. The choice aroma of fellowship with God is dissipated by worldly conversation. Wherefore, come ye out from among them.

December 21

Great men often have petitioners in their halls who will wait for hours, and come again and again to obtain promotion; surely, the God of heaven should be waited for by them that seek him. Thrice happy is he that gets an early interview, and doubly blest is he who gets one at all. Yet it does at times seem hard to stand at a door which opens not to repeated knocking. "I wait for the Lord, my soul doth wait, and in his word do I hope."

December 22

Keep your sail up when there is no wind, that when it blows you may not have need to prepare for it; use means when you see no grace attending them, for thus will you be in the way when grace comes. Better go fifty times and gain nothing than lose one good opportunity. If the angel stir not the pool, yet lie there still, for, it may be, the moment when you leave it will be the season of his descending.

December 23

You wake up one morning, and all the trees are adorned with snowy wreaths, while down below upon the ground the snow lies in a white sheet over everything. Lo, the sun has risen, its beams shed a genial warmth, and in a few hours where is the snow? It has passed away. The Lord acts after the same manner in the new creation: his love shines on the soul, his grace renews us, and the old things pass away as a matter of course.

December 24

When the weather is cold and dreary, we must set a stout heart against the stiff breeze, and determine that if we shiver in body we will be warm in heart. Our thanksgiving for God's mercy is not like a swallow which is gone with the summer; the birds within our bosom sing all the year round. The fire of gratitude will warm us: let us heap on the great logs of loving memories. No cold shall freeze the genial current of our soul; our praise shall flow on when brooks and rivers are bound in chains of ice.

December 25

The joy of Christmas is the meeting of the whole family around the sire. Who cares to spend the day alone? So the richest joys of believers are those which they share with their brethren in Christ, the joys of fellowship with the saints. What a merry-making will it be when the whole of the one family in heaven and earth shall meet in the Father's house above! What joy in each other! What joy in the dear Elder Brother! What joy in God!

December 26

Now and then one finds a daisy peering out amid the grim frost, and answering to its poetic name—"the robin of flowers." How like is this to the happy thoughts of faith, which spring up when the mind is most frostbitten with grief. They are always cheering, and wear a beauty of their own which belongs not to the commoner joys of prosperous times. God forgets us not, however bleak the seasons, but gives us songs in the night and flowers in December.

December 27

We dread the snow, and yet it in very truth warms the earth. "He giveth snow like wool."

> "Earth receives
> Gladly the thickening mantle; and the green
> And tender blade, that feared the chilling blast,
> Escapes unhurt beneath so warm a veil."

Look always upon things which come from God as blessings, and not curses, and you shall find a warm side in them all for which to bless the ever gracious One.

December 28

Love the person of your Lord! Bring forth the alabaster box of your heart, even though it be broken, and let the precious ointment of your love be poured upon his pierced feet. Let your intellect be exercised upon your glorious Lord. Meditate upon what you read concerning him, for the subject deserves all your thoughts. Never was there such a Lover! Love him with your whole being.

December 29

He who trusts in craft, sails this way today, and that way the next, like a vessel tossed about by the fickle wind; but he who trusts in the Lord is like a vessel propelled by steam, which cuts through the waves, defies the wind, and plows one bright, silvery, straightforward track to its destined haven. Be a man with living principles within; be not a slave to the varying customs of this fickle world.

December 30

God makes no difference in his love to his children. A child is a child to him: he will not make him a hired servant, but he shall feast upon the fatted calf, and shall join in the music and the dancing as much as if he had always gladdened his father's heart. When Jesus comes into the heart, he issues a general license to be glad in the Lord. No chains are worn in the court of King Jesus. The admission of believers into full privileges may be gradual, but it is sure.

December 31

Whether you are saved or lost it cannot so much matter to me as it will to you. In the priceless jewel of your own personal immortality you have a far greater interest than any other being can possibly claim. If I faithfully beseech you to look to Jesus, I shall be clear, even if you reject the warning; but, for your own sake, I beseech you to turn to Jesus at once, and find eternal life before the bells ring in another year. By death, which may be so near to you; by judgment, which is so certain to you; by the terror of hell, and by the eternity of its pains; better still, by the sweets of Jesus' love, by the charms of his matchless beauty, by the grace which he is prepared to give, by the heaven whose gates of pearl are glistening before the eye of faith, and by the Lord himself, I entreat you, seek him while he may be found. May his Holy Spirit lead you to do so. Amen.

CPSIA information can be obtained
at www.ICGtesting.com
Printed in the USA
LVHW022218310520
657087LV00002B/492